PETER EVANS and GEOFF DEEHAN

The Keys to Creativity

GRAFTON BOOKS

A Division of the Collins Publishing Group

LONDON GLASGOW
TORONTO SYDNEY AUCKLAND

Grafton Books
A Division of the Collins Publishing Group
8 Grafton Street, London W1X 3LA

Published in paperback by Grafton Books 1990

First published in Great Britain by
Grafton Books 1988

A CIP catalogue record for this
book is available from the British Library

ISBN 0-586-20135-1

Printed and bound in Great Britain by
Collins, Glasgow

Set in Electra

Composition studies for Picasso's *Guernica* reproduced
by courtesy of the Prado, Madrid, © DACS 1988
Guernica reproduced by courtesy of The Bridgeman Art
Library © DACS 1988

As the presenter of .... rogrammes, Peter Evans is one of Britain's best-known science broadcasters and writers. He is the author .... tific, medical and psychological to................................

Geoff Deehan is Editor, Science, for BBC Radio. His particular interests are in the functioning of the brain, and intelligence – both natural and artificial.

Geoff Deehan and Peter Evans are producing a Radio 4 series also entitled *The Keys to Creativity*.

CONTENTS

PREFACE

Writing this book evolved into an unusual experience. We began with the intention of dissecting this much-used word 'creativity' from two angles. First, we set out to investigate the researches, theories and speculations of scientists trying to understand how and why creative people manage to produce works of excellence. Second, we wanted to see how the objective insights of science would match what creative individuals themselves have to say about their achievements: what motivates them; how they organize their thoughts; where ideas come from.

In both cases we were, we thought, on the outside looking in. But researching and writing a book is itself an act of creation. Inevitably, we too became a modest part of the creative population we were studying. We began to find it fruitful to look at 'us' as well as 'them'!

The original idea for the book stemmed from a documentary series on creativity which we were engaged in making for BBC Radio 4. Here, too, was a personal source to mine: namely, how to distil and present the many voices of scientists, artists, psychologists, writers, historians, designers and so on into a coherent, readily-understood broadcast series of programmes.

By thinking reflexively and sounding off our own experiences against those of our many interviewees, we arrived, on tape and on paper, at a surprising conclusion. Perhaps even a creative one.

Our thanks are due to Richard Johnson at Grafton Books for giving us a vehicle for expressing our ideas.

Peter Evans/Geoff Deehan
London 1988

1

THE CREATIVITY CONUNDRUM

First there was the great cosmic egg. Inside the egg was chaos, and floating in chaos was P'an Ku, the Under-developed, the divine Embryo. And P'an Ku burst out of the egg, four times larger than any man today, with a hammer and chisel in his hand with which he fashioned the world.

Third century Chinese myth

Most cultures have their own story of the Creation. Usually an all-powerful supernatural being is described as making the world from the void, fashioning physical reality from what had been until then eternal nothingness or, at best, chaos.

In the biblical version of Genesis, the elaborate process takes just seven days. For today's scientists the Big Bang that initiated time, space and matter – including ourselves – was an instantaneous eruption from the timeless singularity that went before. Both these explanations of the creation of the universe, the religious and the cosmological, are clearly complementary to and compatible with each other. And both rely on some mighty force, presence, power or intention to set the whole cosmos rolling. Here then is, undeniably, an act of creation: from nothing is something, indeed everything, made by the agency of a creator. Here is the pinnacle of creativity. It has also become a universal prototype.

By analogy we have come to regard the process evoked by this much-used, if ill-defined, word 'creativity' as akin in general to a divine act of innovation. The creative person we think of as endowed with quasi-supernatural powers that mysteriously set to work to bring into being works of art or theories in science that are totally new, fresh and original. From nowhere something is materialized. The intermediary – the creator – we call 'gifted' or 'touched with genius'. Consider, for example, these accounts by creative people of the 'creative process' as they see it: ' . . . the germ of composition comes suddenly and unexpectedly. If the soil is ready – that is to say, if the disposition for work is there – it takes root with extraordinary force and rapidity, shoots up through the earth, puts forth branches, leaves and, finally, blossoms.' Or: 'I rely entirely on the unconscious.' And again: ' . . . creation . . . is the activity in which the human mind seems to take least from the outside world, in which it acts or seems to act only of itself and on itself.'

In these brief autobiographical comments we can detect

several key ingredients in the 'inspirational genius' notion of creativity. The first, from the composer Tchaikovsky, embodies the idea of the sudden flash of insight, the 'Aha! Experience'. From out of nowhere, in a manner analogous to the Creation, comes something which the prepared mind goes on to work over into a musical composition. The second, offered by the spectacularly successful advertising man David Ogilvy, treads similar ground. In order to generate what he terms the 'Big Idea', Ogilvy listens to a client's briefing, then leaves it to his unconscious mind to simmer away below the surface in order to come up with a novel thought. Again, a variant on inspirational genius. Third comes the celebrated nineteenth-century French mathematician Henri Poincaré, whose book on the foundations of science contains an attempt to pin down the true nature of scientific and mathematical creativity. Once more the drift of the argument is towards the 'elusive genius' explanation. Poincaré talks a lot about 'intuition', and perceiving 'hidden harmonies and relations', the mysterious emergence from the subliminal self of 'privileged unconscious phenomena'.

Perhaps the most telling advocate of this kind of creative process is Mozart, that extraordinarily prolific composer of enduringly beautiful music who, from time to time, tried to relate to others how he did it. Typically, Mozart wrote in a letter that his ideas flowed most freely when he was alone and in a good mood, say after a satisfying meal. But, he added of these precious ideas, 'Whence and how they come, I know not; nor can I force them.' Having perhaps hummed a melody to himself, Mozart would then go to work on a composition in his head, not piecing it together note by note on paper. Eventually the whole work, even a long one, 'stands almost complete and finished in my mind, so that I can survey it, like a fine picture or a beautiful statue, at a glance'. All the parts of a complete orchestral score are heard, not as a succession of instrumental voices but as a coherent unity, playing together. The final step would be to transfer all this near-finished music from mind to manuscript sheet, like copying a disc on to a cassette. And almost as quick.

In the face of such a description of the creative process it might seem that the inspirational genius case stands proven. For Mozart, writing music was not, apparently, like constructing an edifice brick by brick, rather more like taking dictation from some divine and sublime inner self. In Peter Shaffer's play *Amadeus*, indeed, the jealous, less accomplished Salieri observes that his rival Mozart seems to be composing as if in direct creative communion with God himself.

Can we understand the incomprehensible?

Although the concept of the ill-defined, mysterious, inspired, sublime creative genius has been popular for many centuries, there is some evidence that it is not the end of the story: nor even the beginning or the middle. In fact mysteries quite often evaporate into more hard-nosed phenomena when you investigate them in the right way. Think of how the invention and development of the telescope changed humanity's whole perception of the universe. By being able to look at distant astronomical bodies, we began to see the cosmos not as an earth-centred artefact of the gods, but an extraordinarily big natural machine subject to certain universal laws, motions and interactions. In doing so we did not, and do not, abandon our sense of wonderment at the scale and complexity of the physical world. But we should stop calling events and observations 'mysteries' when what we really mean is that we do not understand them.

So it is with creativity. For many years psychologists tended to treat this particular area of human behaviour as *terra incognita* – unknown territory – that had never been and probably could never be charted. In an address given at

Pennsylvania State College in 1950, the President of the American Psychological Association, J. P. Guilford, chose Creativity as his theme, 'with considerable hesitation, for it represents an area in which psychologists generally, whether they be angels or not, have feared to tread'. Guilford we shall be meeting again later, because he has done much to explore the badlands of creativity. But a few decades ago he was voicing the general apprehensions of behavioural scientists: that creativity is simply not amenable to objective description, analysis, experimentation or inquiry. Like religion or aesthetics, it belongs to a different universe of experience to the motions of planets around stars or the reactions of one chemical with another. Or so it seemed at the time.

Later in his talk Guilford went on to point out how neglected the study of creativity had been. Of approximately 121,000 books and papers listed in *Psychological Abstracts* in the previous 23 years, only 186 seemed, from the index, to have some bearing on the topic of creativity: a mere one-fifth of one per cent. Nearly forty years later the proportion looks decidedly healthier: even so there are still signs that psychologists feel uneasy with the topic. Compared to the numbers of papers published, say, on the differences in thinking abilities between pre-school boys and girls, or the personality traits of lawbreakers, creativity still takes a back seat. However, there have been some outstandingly revealing attempts to pin down the 'mystery' of creativity, and these form the core of this book.

What these investigations suggest most importantly is that the process of creation need not necessarily remain a closed book to the scientific investigator. It is amenable to analysis. As the eminent British scientist Peter Medawar – awarded a Nobel Prize for his exceptional contributions to the study of the immune system – once stated: 'That "creativity" is beyond analysis is a romantic illusion we must now outgrow.'

This conviction finds an echo in the work of Dr Robert

Weisberg, one of the key researchers active in the creativity field whose ideas we shall be exploring in some detail later on. Dr Weisberg too argues that we should jettison the persistent myths that we use to explain the phenomenon of creativity. 'Much of what we believe about creativity,' he writes, 'is not based on hard data but is more or less folklore, passed down from one generation to the next as if it were the truth.'

Clearing the ground

In order to acquire some of that 'hard data' on creativity to which Dr Weisberg refers, it is first necessary to decide precisely what it is that we are going to scrutinize. A straightforward enough ambition you might think, yet, with creativity, hardly a simple one to meet. For one thing, there is no agreement over what constitutes creativity. Certainly it is the sort of thing that people acknowledged as creative do. In the narrowest sense, according to Guilford, 'creativity refers to the abilities that are most characteristic of creative people'. He goes on further in this circular vein with: 'Creative abilities determine whether the individual has the power to exhibit creative behaviour to a noteworthy degree.'

Such definitions beg so many questions that they are hardly satisfactory. It is as if one were to define an electric light bulb as something that lights up when you pass current through it: adequate in a broad sense, but hardly illuminating as a description of the way a bulb uses electricity to generate and scatter light. We need to know more. We need to know, for example, who the creative people are: whether these creative powers are confined, for example, to the superstars of literature, art and science or whether they are shared by more humble folk. Perhaps by us all.

We also need to know more about the personality of the

creative individual. Clearly he or she does possess certain qualities of mind that are brought into service in order to invent, contrive, compose or construct. Are these 'special' qualities or are they in common supply? If the latter, are we then talking about a certain necessary admixture of talents, like a finely balanced chemical formula?

Another series of questions concerns motivation. Creative people tend to work hard at being creative. The French writer Balzac would drive himself relentlessly night after night, sustained by huge (and no doubt unhealthy) amounts of coffee, to revise and complete his novels. Others have a similar inner urge to get things done, to work out of their system a poem, play or painting. Contrary to popular myth, creative people are not fey, ethereal beings waiting to be touched by some fickle muse before setting pen to paper or brush to palette. They work with the intensity, even ferocity, of the beaver to construct the edifices mapped out in their minds. Again, we need to understand the origins of this pressure to create in order truly to understand the process of creation.

A further area that needs clarification is the much-discussed relationship between creativity and intelligence, by which we usually mean an IQ score as derived from an intelligence test. Again we confront a popular misconception. 'Einstein was a genius, an egghead with a telephone number IQ.' 'Sure Picasso was creative. He was a very bright guy, wasn't he?' 'Shakespeare? A creative genius, with an IQ you couldn't measure.' Such comments are typical. Of course creative people are intelligent, runs the argument, therefore the first-leaguers – the 'genius' types – are ultra-intelligent. The logic is inescapable. But it is false. As we shall see later, there is little or no connection between adult IQ and creative achievement beyond a certain level. This baseline is not a stratospheric score of 160 or 180 but a mere 120 – bright but not outstandingly so. As a predictor of creativity, then, an IQ score is limited. And the reason seems to be that intelligence tests themselves measure intellectual skills that, compared to creative skills, are too limited. In short, creativity demands a certain base level of intelligence, not the highest IQ scores. This might seem to be something of a paradox, which indeed it is. It is possible for a person not unduly gifted with exceptional intelligence to be the creator of superlative or sublime works of extraordinary power and insight. A composer may be a prodigy as a child but perform quite averagely in the classroom on the three Rs among peers with no creative talent, or at least none that has become apparent.

A conundrum wrapped in a paradox

Those sparkling individuals whom we all agree are or were exceptionally creative turn out often to be quite unexceptional in all other respects. Not only are they not particularly bright when measured on a modern IQ test, they seem only averagely artistic or cerebral or perceptive in their personalities in general, compared to the rest of the population.

Think, say, of Shakespeare. He was, in terms of background and education, no one very special. Not the scion of some illustrious literary family. Not a privileged member of Elizabethan society. He was, in fact, a very practical sort of character, a theatrical tradesman almost, running a theatre, dealing with the frustrations and trivia of everyday business matters. What is more he was obliged by the nature of his job to produce at short notice, like today's newsroom scriptwriters, lines that would be easy to deliver by his actors. No doubt the deadline pressures kept him in a highly adrenalized frame of mind. But you would not think that this was the sort of life-style conducive to generating a superabundance of plays and verse universally acknowledged to be of supreme power and beauty.

Here then is a true conundrum: and it is not confined to William Shakespeare but characterizes creative people in general. What is there in a person that enables him or her to transcend the intellectual, emotional or expressive boundaries that restrict the rest of us, to produce work of true creativity?

The rest of this book is an attempt to answer that perennially fascinating question.

2

TOWARDS A DEFINITION OF CREATIVITY

Creativity is one of those things that is much easier to detect than to define.

Stephen Bayley, design historian

Before long we are going to have to bite the bullet, metaphorically speaking, and define this evocative word 'creativity', in itself no mean task because there are probably a few hundred definitions at least from which to choose. According to the American psychiatrist Dr John G. Young, we can approach the difficult problem of defining creativity from two directions.

First, there is the product of creation. Creativity, in this context, is what creative people do. We use intelligence and the imagination to make up something new, fresh and lasting, transforming the old into something better. The creator, writes Dr Young, 'surpasses the traditional with the innovative, the outmoded with an improvement'.

An alternative to this kind of definition is one based on the Greek verb *krainein* which means 'to fulfil'. Creativity here, argues Young, is what creative people are. 'As we transcend our past in the things we do, we also become who we can be. Thus creativity is those attitudes by which we fulfil ourselves.' Now this variant is a very important one because it embraces within the phrase 'creative individual' far more people than those who work in obviously 'creative' fields, such as art or research or inventing things. It also owes a lot to the psychologist Abraham Maslow who gave us the term 'self-actualization' to describe the fulfilment, or actualization, of our true potential.

Thus, by this definition, anyone who fulfils his or her potential, who expresses an inner drive or capacity, who strikes out into unknown psychological territory, may be said to be creative. Furthermore, this kind of creativity is not inferior to the widely recognized kind which generates fine sculptures or stylish sonatas. As Maslow put it most succinctly: 'It is better to make a first-rate soup than a second-rate painting.'

A gift or a skill?

Whichever general definition one takes – the narrow 'output' notion or the broad personal 'potential' idea – the question then arises of whether creative individuals are naturally gifted with their capacity or are exercising an acquired skill. Setting aside for a moment the sublimities of a Leonardo da Vinci painting or a Beethoven symphony – so easy to attribute to an innate gift – consider Maslow's first-rate soup maker or a 'green-fingered' gardener. Both have learned a trade that anyone might emulate from reading the right books and talking to informed people. Yet both seem to have something extra – an 'X' factor – in their work that gives them an edge. The excellent cook has an unerring feel for what tastes exactly right, even though he or she has access to no special ingredients. The talented gardener, given soil, seed and growing conditions that are accessible to the rest of us, still manages to nurture plants that surpass the norm. Are we witnessing here some kind of quasi-magical gift? Are the hands of the chef or the gardener the instruments of something beyond and above simply a refined skill?

Most attempts to understand creativity in the past have tended to favour the 'gift' scenario. It has been estimated that, of all those who have ever lived throughout history, only about two in a million were really distinguished in their field. If one eliminates from this select list people who owed their distinction to the vagaries of fortune or historical accident, as well as those whose achievements were not strictly speaking creative in the senses that we have been using the term, that means that creativity appears but very rarely among us. That fact alone has suggested that creative individuals are a lucky, chosen few endowed with a precious gift by a random spin of the genetic wheel of fortune.

The implication of this line of reasoning is that creativity comes ready made and free at birth with all one's other characteristics such as hair or eye colour, nose shape, skin tones and so on. A free gift from which one can benefit. A gift from a friendly muse who, during the course of one's life, will choose to visit the suitable individual to trigger off a creative production. The birth of this idea is certainly understandable and its survival seems assured, but only among those who have not bothered to look closely enough at how creativity works in practice. Both creative people themselves and behavioural scientists studying the process by which they create now agree that creativity involves a highly developed skill in bringing into being new, original, valuable ideas or products.

Support for this point of view comes from a variety of sources. Take for a start those little parlour games and puzzles designed to test one's creative thinking abilities. Look at one such typical problem illustrated below. Arrange some matchsticks according to the diagram. The test is to move just three matches to form four squares, making sure that all the matches are used. On page 37 is the correct solution. Now success in this and hundreds of similar puzzles depends on making a genuine creative leap: by thinking that the squares

PROBLEM I

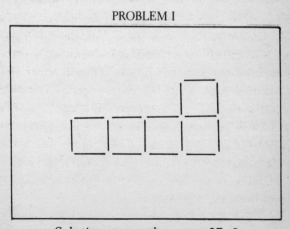

Solutions to puzzles on pp. 37–8

do not have to be attached to each other as they are in the original configuration. If you had, as most people do, an unconscious assumption that the squares must be contiguous, then you have to discard it. You have to avoid jumping to the obvious, automatic route to a solution.

However, although this may, at a certain level, be called 'creative thinking', it is really akin to any other skill that you might learn. Look again at the matchsticks and try now to form four squares by moving only two sticks. By now you will have been mentally primed to make a second creative leap, in order to reach the correct solution (see page 37).

Once again it is a question of discarding an automatic assumption, this time that all the squares are of the same size. Unless one does this there is no hope of reaching a new or original solution because one will simply run around in intellectual circles, unable to break out of the tramlines imposed by one's preconceptions. As the psychologist Dr David Taylor remarks: 'The essence of creativity . . . is the ability to take a fresh look at familiar objects and situations, enriched by past experience but not constrained by it.'

Below is yet another matchstick problem. Try to solve it, again by discarding strategies or methods that you find will

PROBLEM II

A bigger challenge: move just one match so that the equation is
balanced

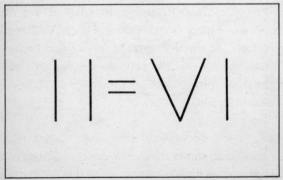

not work. (Solution on page 38.) If you got anywhere near to a correct solution (and this is not an easy problem), then you should have no difficulty with the problem below. Connect the nine dots by drawing just four straight lines, and without lifting pen from paper. (Solution page 38.)

PROBLEM III

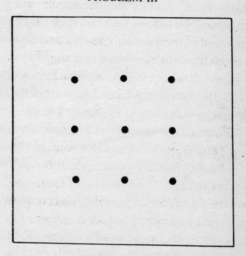

What is true of the apparently trivial pursuits of match-sticks and pen-and-paper puzzles, is also valid for more complex and elevated acts of creativity. If one delves more carefully for example into the thoughts of Tchaikovsky, whom we saw earlier as an exponent of the 'Aha!' method of composition, we see that even he argues that the so-called 'gift' is not free. It needs to be earned. In a letter written in 1878, he shows himself a champion of the perspiration – not inspiration – method of working:

There is no doubt that even the greatest musical geniuses have sometimes worked without inspiration. This guest does not always respond to the first invitation.

We must *always* work, and a self-respecting artist must not fold his hands in the pretext that he is not in the mood.

There can be few creative individuals who do not share Tchaikovsky's sentiments. Painters and writers, not surprisingly when you think about it, often report that they get up in the mornings feeling like the rest of us: a bit dull or listless, not really enthusiastic about the thought of work. Because they have fixed working hours – again like most of us – they set to, however, putting words on paper or paint on canvas. There is no scintillating muse jolting their mood or intellect into action, no automatic pilot guiding their hand towards a creative end. Simply careful, scrupulous, laborious work. Sometimes the creative individual has to fight to concentrate on the task in hand, just as many of us have to struggle to keep our mind on the job and off an impending lunch or dinner date.

Little that can be termed creative happens by accident. It takes application and determination. A million monkeys banging away randomly at the keys of a million typewriters may, in a million years, eventually type out the whole of Shakespeare's plays. Such serendipity is not inconceivable. But human beings do not have the benefit of those colossal timescales for their writing activities. More to the point, the energetic monkey would certainly not recognize that he and his associates had succeeded in producing anything coherent, let alone important. The skill of composition is not just in generating words, images or ideas but in selectively recognizing the useful and discarding the dross.

In his perceptive chapter 'The Making of a Poem' (in the symposium *The Creative Process*, 1946) the poet Stephen Spender – himself acknowledged as a highly creative artist – shows from his own work how much skill, judgement, application and concentration are required to produce a valuable poem. Spender points out that poets, like composers, work in different ways. One creates a poem in a rapid burst – or so it seems. Others are plodders.

> Some poets write immediately works which, when they are written scarcely need revision. Others write their poems by stages, feeling their way from rough draft to rough draft, until finally, after many revisions, they have produced a result which may seem to have very little connection with their early sketches.

A musical analogy might be the difference between Mozart and Beethoven. The former seemed to work out in his head entire symphonies or operatic scenes before writing them down. His manuscripts show remarkably little correction or revision. No wonder Salieri might have thought that Mozart was taking dictation from God. Beethoven on the other hand was, comparatively speaking, a 'plodder', constantly jotting themes and sketches into notebooks, reworking and developing musical concepts over many years. When researchers began to study those notebooks they were amazed at some of the entries. What ended up as sublime music began as fairly crude and unattractive early drafts. Clearly Beethoven had fashioned his original, unsatisfactory raw material with immense creative skill, returning and improving over many years.

Actually the distinction between the apparently 'inspired genius' Mozart and the more pedestrian Beethoven is nothing like as clear-cut as it may seem. Detailed study of the output of Mozart shows that here too was a careful and meticulous worker, marshalling his resources economically and skilfully, borrowing themes from here and there, never wasting those ideas that came to him. Although he had a rare ability to hear a complex composition in its entirety in his head before committing it to paper (and this he did very quickly), Mozart himself describes how he put together ideas collected in his memory, humming them to himself and imposing on them the variations of counterpoint, say, or trying out different combinations of instruments. In short, the notebooks are there, real enough, for Mozart as for Beethoven: but they are notebooks of the mind.

Stephen Spender describes himself as an inveterate jotter. Beside his desk he keeps at least twenty notebooks containing rough sketches, ideas for poems, single lines, anything relevant to his art. In reconstructing a particular, finished idea we can see that, for Spender at least, poetry-writing is not just a matter of taking inspired dictation. It is clearly hard work. He would begin, for example, with what seems like a perfectly acceptable and undeniably expressive line and a half:

> . . . The waves
> Like wires burn with the sun's copper glow.

Because this phrase is central to the whole message of the poem in which it occurs, Spender worried a lot about it. Indeed, he composed many versions of that same passage, while the whole poem went through at least twenty drafts. Finally he was satisfied with:

> Afternoon gilds all the silent wires
> Into a burning music of the eyes

To get from the prototype to the finished product, Spender exerts an enormous amount of effort. He will try using a verb from one version as an adjective in another. He will see what effect the word 'trembling' has instead of 'burning'. He sketches out 'a golden music in the eyes', then 'music golden to the eyes' before dropping the word 'golden' altogether and containing its sense in the verb 'gilds' and so on. It is painstaking, trial-and-error composition in which new variants are constantly being put forward and judged for their effectiveness in the overall context of the poem. Only when the various pieces 'fit' in a complex mosaic of imagery, does Spender consider the poem finished. That too is an act of judgement: knowing when to stop.

The nature of novelty

Isaac Newton is often singled out as the most brilliantly innovative and creative scientist of all time – a megastar among many other brilliant luminaries. His celebrated *Principia* was a masterly work in which Newton described in precise mathematical – that is genuinely scientific – terms the motions of bodies in space and their interactions. Still today space scientists acknowledge they are drawing on the *Principia* when they plan moonshots or calculate planetary motions. The astounding weight of scientific research since Newton's death in 1727 – especially Albert Einstein's revolutionary theories – has not dented his reputation as one of the all-time elite; an original thinker *par excellence*. Interestingly enough, though, Newton himself recognized that he did not develop his ideas in an intellectual vacuum. 'If I have been able to see farther than others,' he wrote, 'it is because I have stood on the shoulders of giants.'

Newton's sense of his historical context was both perceptive and well-founded. Before him there had indeed been gigantic intellects trying to make sense of the physical world: indeed it is possible to trace a complete lineage of ideas back to and even beyond the ancient Greeks who, like Newton, had wondered at the properties and behaviour of heavenly bodies. Such exercises in intellectual genealogy can be applied to any other creative individual one cares to name. Shakespeare, for example, drew freely for his plots on other writers, living or dead. He also exploited to the full the dramatic devices and conventions commonly used by contemporary Elizabethan dramatists. Sometimes creativity is not so much building on existing ways of doing things, as breaking with convention. Without the formal, cool elegance of Augustan classicism there might never have been the sensuous emotional output of Romantics such as Byron or Keats. Without the somewhat predictable plots, characters and themes of post-war British theatre, John Osborne and the restless and protesting 'angry young men' might never have found their innovative means of self-expression.

However, whether the creative individual is modifying and enhancing the techniques or methods common to his or her day or deliberately setting out to create a revolution, a sense of history, of working within and through those that have gone before, is essential. It is this that forms the basis for innovation as opposed to repetition or sterility. So far as creative work is concerned, never was it truer that 'Those who cannot remember the past are condemned to repeat it.'

Now this in itself does not explain the creativity of a Shakespeare, a Newton or a Wordsworth. It does not tell us how one person, standing on the shoulders of his intellectual forerunners, should stand out so conspicuously from his contemporaries, given precisely the same intellectual or artistic heritage. However, it does further undermine the concept of creativity as an out-of-the-blue phenomenon, owing nothing to circumstance and everything to individual 'genius' or 'inspiration'. It also points up the important distinction between novelty pure and simple and innovation with originality – which is what creativity is all about.

Originality: an essential ingredient

Newness and originality are both necessary to give a work or a theory the mark of distinction. Plenty of writers, composers or scientists come up with novel thoughts. Novel, that is, to them. It happens all the time. Indeed it happens to all of us. Sometimes when we are in a relaxed frame of mind, out walking perhaps or soaking in a bath tub, images or imaginings come to us: snatches of dialogue between ourselves and a fictional character perhaps; or an ingenious explanation for an everyday phenomenon. Or we might recollect a vivid dream in which we came up with a blinding insight or a 'secret of the universe'. Disappointingly, these great or imaginative thoughts rarely seem to have any staying power. What is more they have an embarrassing habit, when we look more closely at them, of being not original at all, but quite commonplace. Many people have had the thought before.

To make something new – in the sense of being different from what went before – can be, when you try it, surprisingly easy. Anyone, with the randomness of a monkey hitting the keys of a typewriter, can generate novelty. Suppose for example you were asked to compose a modern poem on the theme of the sea. Without too much difficulty you might jot down and string together a series of words and images, along these lines:

> Waves leap.
> Foam surges,
> Sparkling,
> Brilliant in the summer sun.

Without needing to conform to the constraints of rhyme or metre you could quickly compose quite a long and no doubt impressive piece of free verse. It would certainly be new, in the sense that your combination of words – unless there were an unlikely coincidence – would be unique to you alone.

What a glibly concocted work of this kind would lack in many cases (not all) would be the originality that comes from exerting the particular skill of the true poet. As Stephen Spender writes:

> Night, dark, stars, immensity, blue, voluptuous, cling-ing, columns, clouds, moon, sickle, harvest, vast camp fire, hell. Is this poetry? A lot of strings of words almost as simple as this are set down on the backs of envelopes and posted off to editors or to poets by the vast array of amateurs who think that to be illogical is to be poetic, with that question.

Almost invariably the answer is 'No'. Such efforts are like the drawings made by children of cars, horses or giraffes that their parents pin proudly to the wall as indicative of the artistic prowess of their offspring. Undoubtedly these bold and carefree sketches are new for the child, exploring through paint or crayon an exciting environment. But they are, at the same time, hardly innovative. They resemble thousands of similar efforts by children of the same age, all of whom are seeing and representing their world in much the same way.

What links the naïve child to the inexpert poet is that neither has any proper context for the work. They behave as if what they are doing is being done for the very first time, as if re-inventing the wheel. Again we are back to recognizing one's context. This does not necessarily mean that to be original one has to strive to produce excessively elaborate variations of what has gone before. It may mean, as T. F. Wolff explains in an article on 'The Many Masks of Modern Art', no more than seeing something with unprecedented clarity. 'One of the most original of all works of art, Albrecht Dürer's "The Young Hare", resulted from nothing more unusual than an artist looking very, very carefully at a young animal, and then trying his very best to draw it exactly as it appeared.' Today, Wolff goes on to point out, we would, particularly in the era of the camera, see such a drawing as very photographic and therefore unoriginal: simply a slavish copy of nature. 'But, in its time and place, it was a truly revolutionary act.'

Implicit in this view of originality is the notion that the creative individual is a skilful bender or breaker of rules. He or she is able to take existing conventions or methods or theories and transcend them. We see this time and time again. One conspicuous example is the work of one of the greatest creative musicians of this century, the jazz trumpeter Louis Armstrong. Here was a young man learning music and playing it professionally like many others of his generation – school brass bands then, later, in the honky-tonks and bordellos of New Orleans. The style of music, though fairly new, was nevertheless established. A group of players, often trumpet, trombone, clarinet, piano, rhythm guitar or bass and drums, would take a theme such as a blues or a street march, and improvise variations in concert and individually.

Now there were undoubtedly many talented and well-schooled trumpeters playing jazz when Armstrong came on the scene but, suddenly, he began to find a new kind of musical 'voice'. He would, instead of hitting notes on a regular beat, lag behind a little (or a lot) to give added tension and drama to his solos. He would exploit a wider range of musical 'colour' from his instrument so that it acquired a distinctive, recognizable tone. He began, in short, to explore the edges of his musical context and thereby expand its boundaries. With each new solo he seemed to break fresh ground as his confidence and skill developed. In a few short years he seemed almost to have redefined the term 'jazz' in the same way that Picasso changed our concept of 'painting' or James Joyce our view of the 'novel'.

In all these cases, without the norms and conventions that for others might have been restricting or sterile, their achievements would have been impossible. Indeed one way in which we might measure creative achievement is by assessing the distance between something which is conventional and that which is original.

Another ingredient we have to consider at the same time is the value of a piece of creative work.

Value judgements

A person may succeed in skilfully manipulating words, images or mathematical symbols to produce something that is undeniably original, according to the criteria we have just discussed. But that something may not show any great degree of creativity because it lacks value. To be valuable a product must be recognized as such by a number of people. It must have general appeal, universality and durability. Creativity is often compared to a rare and precious substance such as gold or diamonds. These are internationally recognized as valuable, not least because they are relatively scarce. On another planet in another galaxy the most precious commodities might be stone or cow dung. However we should not confuse *rarity* – which is an extrinsic accident – with intrinsic *value*. Creativity owes its value to the importance of its products, not because it is in short supply. It may not be like hard-to-get minerals at all. Quite the opposite. Indeed, as we shall see later in this book, there is overwhelming evidence that there is no shortage of creativity all around us. It is superabundant, though we do not always know how to prospect for, mine and exploit it. That does not make it any less valuable.

Assessing the value of creative output can be very difficult because it comes in different varieties and guises. As Dr John Young points out, many works of art have value only to their creator. Others may regard them as of little value in recording and expressing human experience.

A housewife paints a scene of a mountain with a lake in front of it. It has value to her because it reminds her of a pleasant time at the cabin last summer. To others it may have no intrinsic aesthetic value. They may pass it off as 'calendar art'. When people suffering from severe psychological disturbance such as schizophrenia express some of their inner turmoil in paintings, the result is often valuable to the patient but not to all observers. Some may find these pictures exceedingly moving. Others fail to be touched by them. In this very ambivalence of response, it may be argued, the schizophrenic derives value because he or she . . . is an ambivalent personality.

In both these cases the value of what is creative remains highly localized to one or just a few people. It is hardly, in Dr Young's words, 'a desirable enlargement of the human experience'.

Then there are those examples of creativity that seem to have varied in value with the passage of time. One such fluctuater is the prolific eighteenth-century composer Johann Sebastian Bach. Today Bach is held in the highest esteem. His works – many hundreds of them – are frequently performed around the world, and in any record store his recordings occupy a sizeable shelf space. However, after Bach died in 1750, it was, for nearly three-quarters of a century, as if he had never lived. His music was simply ignored and not revived until the nineteenth century. Even then, when it was performed, it was usually played in an inappropriate style, and certainly a long way from the baroque sound that the composer originally conceived. So often what we now regard as the supreme artistry of a Bach fugue has been treated as a kind of mechanical exercise in musical competence. So often the composer of the immensely moving Mass in B minor or numerous sublime cantatas was thought of as superficial or glib. He was written off as having no emotional depth or breadth, as having no value.

Clearly the music itself does not change over the years. What has endowed Bach with value is changing tastes and perceptions among his listeners. The intrinsic beauty of his music lay unappreciated until the ears of audiences and critics were attuned to a different aesthetic wavelength.

In science, also, there are many examples of a valuable idea or theory being ignored or even suppressed altogether initially, only to emerge in its true colours later on. When Galileo, by dint of straightforward observation and recording of data, suggested that the earth revolved around its parent star the sun and was not the centre of the universe, he was condemned as a heretic. When quantum theory first suggested that the physical world was not necessarily determined by laws and principles that allow you to predict how matter is going to behave, lots of scientists themselves felt uncomfortable. Instead of dealing with certainties they now had to live with the hazy, unsatisfactory concept of probabilities. It was a disturbing omission. Even Einstein was moved to comment on those new and revolutionary theories: 'God does not play dice.'

When Charles Darwin proposed that humans were just like all other animals, the products of an evolutionary process and therefore with primitive ancestors, many of his contemporaries frowned, scoffed and criticized because, again, here was an unacceptable overturning of conventional wisdom. Today, although there are a few dissenters on the fringe, all these ideas are part of the common stock of science. They are some of its essential conceptual building blocks. They, like the foundation stones of any edifice, have irreplaceable value. But it was not always so.

Recognizing what is of value is not always easy. But it is essential to the process of creation. A Bach or a Darwin has to appreciate the value of what he is doing and not be deflected by others from sticking to a conviction. In other words, to be creative a person needs not only 'creative abilities' such as we have been discussing in this chapter, but also qualities of personality and determination to realize his or her objectives. In the next chapter we shall explore these qualities in greater detail.

SOLUTION IA

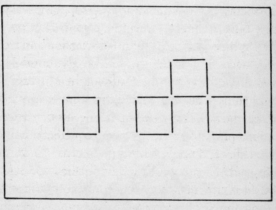

SOLUTION IB

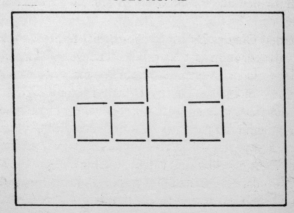

SOLUTION II

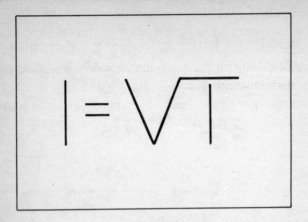

SOLUTION III

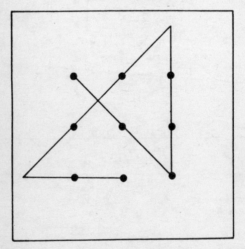

Summary

1 · Creativity and creative ways of thinking are skills that can be developed and refined.

2 · Conscious application is needed, not the vagaries of 'inspiration', in order to achieve a creative output.

3 · Creative people tend to view their work in its cultural, intellectual or historical context.

4 · Originality is not novelty for its own sake.

5 · To qualify for the description 'creative' a product must have inherent value.

3

MEASURING THE MYSTERY

Earlier in this book we touched on the circular definition of creativity – it is what creative people do. But are there any other attributes that are common to creative individuals? Or any ways of assessing who will, or will not, be creative? In this chapter we will look at attempts to measure creativity, some of the theories that have been proposed to explain it, and efforts to gain insights into the characters of those who appear to have it.

One of the most confused questions in the subject is: do you have to be intelligent to be creative? The short answer appears to be: with caution, no. There is no direct correlation between any of the ways we have for measuring intelligence and the ability to create. This is not to say that intelligence is not required for creativity. Rather it appears that, within certain bounds, the absolute magnitude of your intelligence doesn't really matter. As the British psychologist Liam Hudson points out: 'A mature scientist with an adult IQ of 130 is as likely to win a Nobel Prize as is one whose IQ is 180.' Indeed the scientist of high renown, argues Hudson, is typically the 'B+' student. As a predictor of creativity then, an IQ score is limited. And the reason seems to be that intelligence tests themselves measure intellectual skills that, compared to creative behaviour, are too limited. Hudson offers a telling analogy, with IQ tests and spelling tests: 'A man who cannot spell at all cannot write a novel. But once his ability to spell reaches a certain level, the restrictions which his inability impose on him largely disappear.' He goes on to point out that Scott Fitzgerald for one was an atrocious speller, while Einstein, in the same way, was comparatively a 'mediocre' mathematician, and Darwin 'virtually innumerate'.

This might seem to be something of a paradox, which indeed it is. It is possible for a person not gifted with exceptional intelligence to be the creator of superlative or sublime works of extraordinary power and insight. A composer may be a prodigy as a child, but perform quite averagely in the classroom on the three Rs among peers who have no creative talent, or at least none that has become apparent.

In sum – or some – then, it appears that it ain't what you got, it's the way that you use it that matters. Above a certain level, at least. Naïvety, or the ability to throw off adult censorship and preconceptions, has been implicated in the creative process from every direction. There are many cases of naïve creation – the child who produces beautiful music, or fine poetry. One of the most recent is Stephen Wiltshire.

Stephen is autistic: he finds it very difficult to communicate with the outside world. By the age of thirteen he was able, though, to produce drawings, principally of buildings, of great clarity and beauty. It must be said, however, that his skill appears to be that of the draughtsman. His pictures are complete in every detail, but so far they are limited to pure representations of the scene before him. As he grows older will he start to create his own visions? We shall see. If he does then this will undermine still further the notion that 'intelligence' and creativity are synonymous.

Don't get smart, get creative

If sheer bulk number-crunching neural power is not the key, then, what might be? There are almost as many theories as there are people who have studied the problem. Some key notions have emerged which have so far stood the test of time, albeit with modifications. They include:

The unconscious

The unconscious mind has fascinated those interested in the source of ideas.

The French mathematician Henri Poincaré described how after many days of fruitless thought about a problem in mathematics, the solution came to him in a flash of insight as he boarded the steps of a bus. For Poincaré, the unconscious is a melting-pot in which all the experiences, memories, ideas, in fact all the mental life of the creator, can be combined and recombined until something worthwhile emerges. Poincaré believed that a certain amount of editing took place in the unconscious. Only those ideas which might have some relevance, or which seem to possess the beauty so beloved of mathematicians, make it through the veil to the conscious mind. There they are subjected to the full analytical – and necessarily restrictive – powers of the mind.

A more complex view was proposed by Sigmund Freud. Freud separated thought into two distinct kinds. Primary-process thought is unconscious. It operates outside the bounds of logic and rationality. Secondary-process thought operates consciously. It is subject to all the controls imposed by our conscious minds.

In the unconscious scheme of things, it is primary-process thought which generates ideas. It is unconscious and uncontrolled. It is hence able to make seemingly nonsensical connections, to play with novel ideas, to look at the world in fresh ways. Freud also held the view that dreams are mediated by primary-process thought – hence the supposed creative power of dreams. Once an idea becomes established in the unconscious, it can then transfer to the conscious mind. This sudden cross-over has been invoked to explain the flashes of inspiration in which ideas sometimes seem to arrive.

Others have built on and elaborated Freud's central notion. Arthur Koestler suggested that the roots of creativity lie in what he called 'bisociation', the combining of concepts that were previously unrelated: they may, in fact, even be opposites. Koestler himself puts it so in his book *The Act of Creation*:

I have coined the term 'bisociation' in order to make a distinction between the routine skills of thinking on a single 'plane', as it were, and the creative act, which, as I shall try to show, always operates on more than one plane. The former may be called single-minded, the latter a double-minded, transitory state of unstable equilibrium where the balance of both emotion and thought is disturbed.

Koestler quotes the example of Gutenberg and the invention of the printing press. Gutenberg knew that letters could be transferred to paper by carving them in wooden blocks. The wooden blocks were then inked. Paper was placed over them, and the back of the paper was rubbed. The ink adhered to the paper. So far so good, but the prospect of carving the 1300 or so pages of the Bible into wooden blocks was daunting. How to find a more efficient method?

Gutenberg had also seen that the seals used on documents committed information to paper, and could be used many times over. And he had realized that the process of stamping out coins could in principle be used to impart letters to pieces of metal. But one piece was still missing. The answer appeared from an unlikely source: 'I took part in the wine harvest. I watched the wine flowing, and going back from the effect to the cause, I studied the power of the press which nothing can resist' (*The Act of Creation*).

Gutenberg saw immediately that the same pressure can be used to impress a coin or a seal – made out of lead which is easy to work – on to paper: 'A simple substitution which is a ray of light . . . To work then! God has revealed to me the secret that I demanded of him . . . I have had a large quantity of lead brought to my house and that is the pen with which I shall write' (*ibid.*).

For Koestler, the ray of light was the bisociation of the wine press and the seal. He interprets this as the essence of creativity, the bringing together of concepts from different sources in the unconscious mind until a novel idea is produced.

Several psychoanalysts since Freud have proposed similar schemes. Ernst Kris split creativity into two phases – the inspirational and the elaborational. During inspiration logic loses control and unconscious thought processes come into operation. Ideas are combined without the inhibitions imposed by the conscious mind. During the later, elaborational phases, logic again takes control and evaluates the worth of the ideas generated during inspiration.

The role of the unconscious has recently come under attack. In his book *Creativity*, the psychologist Robert Weisberg attempts to lay what he calls 'The Myth of the Unconscious'. Weisberg considers the evidence for unconscious incubation of ideas in the cases of Poincaré, Mozart, Coleridge and Kekulé. All these people are supposed to have had ideas come to them in flashes of inspiration: Mozart wrote his music straight down without revisions; Poincaré obtained his mathematical insight while stepping on to a bus; Coleridge was given his poem *Kubla Khan* in a dream brought on by opium; Kekulé perceived the structure of the chemical benzene as a ring in a dream in which he saw a serpent eating its own tail.

Weisberg's analysis casts considerable doubt on these reports. In the case of Coleridge, for example, it turns out that an earlier version of the poem exists. Mozart's notebooks do contain finished compositions, but also unfinished works which were revised at a later stage of the creative process. In conclusion, Weisberg attacks the notion that leaps of insight are the result of a person suddenly becoming conscious of a previously unconscious idea:

There are now a number of reasons to doubt the occurrence of such leaps of thought . . . First, such leaps are difficult, if not impossible, to demonstrate under controlled conditions. Second, many of the reports on which the unconscious theory is based are of questionable accuracy . . . one could say that the burden of proof now falls on those who propose subjective reports as support for a theory of unconscious processes in creative thinking.

Another voice of dissent comes from the behavioural scientist Howard Gruber, who sees creation as the result of conscious thought, unconscious thinking playing no major role. Gruber finds it unsurprising that when the creative individual 'bends all his efforts toward some great goal, the same problems which occupy his rational waking thoughts will shape his imagery and pervade his dreams'. He suggests that there is first a preparatory phase, in which all the appropriate information is actively sought and analysed. This is followed by a second phase in which 'when the paths of previously independent systems intersect, the result is something new, not predictable from our knowledge of the special laws governing each system in isolation'. There is something of the 'flash of insight' idea of creativity here, but Gruber is more subtle.

He believes that you have to work at it: 'The process of discovery is . . . complex, extended over time, and the collective result of several efforts in which understanding is successfully deepened.'

There have been attempts to unlock artificially the supposed unconscious powers of creativity. In the early 1960s a Los Angeles psychiatrist called Oscar Janigar conducted an experiment to see if the hallucinogenic drug LSD could help – or hinder – painters. Each subject was asked to paint a picture of an American Indian doll before and after taking the drug. There was enormous difference between the two results. Without the drug, the artists tended to draw lifelike representations of the doll. But under the influence of LSD they produced flamboyant, abstract paintings, filling all the space available to them. Janigar suggests that the drug allowed the artists to gain access to buried – unconscious – forms of expression. Each artist could in principle paint in any number of ways. In practice they tended to use a limited repertoire of styles. LSD stimulated them to use means of expression they had been unaware of previously. The artists in this study all valued the experience, and thought that it had had a positive effect on their work. Unfortunately, LSD is now illegal.

Where, then, stands the unconscious? At the moment, its role in creative thought must be judged not proved. We will be looking again at the unconscious generation of thoughts from a physiological point of view in Chapter 6.

Associations

Sarnoff Mednick, a psychologist at the University of Southern California, has worked extensively on theories of creativity. (He is also, by the way, interested in the workings of the criminal mind, which might be no coincidence.) Mednick believes creativity is: 'the forming of associative elements into new combinations which either meet specified requirements or are in some way useful'. In other words, the creative process is driven by associations between ideas. The more ideas people have in their heads, and the greater the number of associations they can form between them, then the more creative they will be.

One implication of this view is that there is no such thing as a novel idea except one arrived at by chance. Association-ism requires that problems are solved and works of art generated by the transfer of existing ideas to new surround-ings. Obviously, for associationism to work, every problem which is capable of solution must have similarities to other problems which have already been solved. And the emergence of previously unseen concepts can only come about by the random juggling of existing ideas into new forms.

In 1945, Jacques Hadamard, a French mathematician, published the results of his own study into creativity in mathematics. His ideas bear strong similarities to associationism, but with an added dash of input from the psychiatrists. For Hadamard, creativity proceeds through four stages. In the first, preparation, the problem to be solved is addressed in a logical fashion. This takes place consciously. In the second, incubation, the outcome of the preparatory stage is allowed to ripen in the unconscious. New combinations of ideas are generated, possibly randomly, but, as in his countryman Poincaré's theory, most do not reach consciousness. Only when the unconscious mind recognizes something worthwhile, during the third stage of illumination, does it allow it to feed through to consciousness. Here, in the fourth stage of verification, exposition and utilization, the creative product is stated systematically, and tested against the problem it is supposed to solve.

There are anecdotes which seem to support in practice the idea of associationism. Most recently, Graham Woyka, a mathematician and chemical engineer, created a new and much more efficient way to store information in a computer. His starting-point was not a rigorous analysis of how data might be compressed. Rather, he had become interested in the linguistic richness of metaphor in Greek drama. He realized that although the number of words in the vocabulary is limited, the number of ideas which can be expressed with them is unlimited. Having made the crucial conceptual link between drama and data processing, Woyka went on to build a prototype machine that can process the equivalent of a Bible in three seconds by encoding data with the compressive efficiency of figurative language.

Woyka's advance is not an engineering achievement in the narrow technical sense – he did not just build a faster computer. It is rather an advance in idea manipulation, a new concept created from the marriage of two seemingly unrelated fields.

Madness

In the 1890s the playwright August Strindberg underwent an extreme attack of mental illness. Psychiatrists have since diagnosed it as paranoid schizophrenia. He believed he was being attacked through the walls of his room with poison gas and electricity. He believed himself to be assailed by flies covered in red spots. He heard voices. Yet he also produced some of his best work during the period.

It is quite easy to believe that genius and madness have common roots. Our perception of the genius is usually that of someone outside society. Someone who does not adhere to social norms. Someone whose thoughts go their own way, frequently into realms that normal people find uncomfortable or incomprehensible. Someone prone to mercurial changes of mood. We also tend to consider many of these attributes to be characteristic of lunacy. The connection between madness and creativity has been – and still is – the subject of vigorous debate.

In 1976, Hans and Sybil Eysenck published a book with the title *Psychoticism as a Dimension of Personality*, in which they argued that creative people also have many of the characteristics of psychotic behaviour. Recently, Kay Jamison, a psychologist at the University of California, Los Angeles, claims to have found evidence that poets in particular suffer from manic depression. Jamison believes that the violent oscillation in mood between depression and elation undergone by manic depressives may actually help the process of creation.

Anthony Storr, the British psychiatrist who has studied the phenomenon for many years, defines the relationship thus in his book *The Dynamics of Creation*: 'Creativity is one mode adopted by gifted people of coming to terms with, or finding symbolic solutions for, the internal tensions and dissociations from which all human beings suffer in varying degree.' This may be one reason why Strindberg never actually succumbed to his madness – his art provided a mechanism through which he could disperse his mental difficulties. Storr goes on: 'What is unusual about the creative person is that he has easy access to his inner world, and does not repress it as much as most people. When he is able to create, he certainly is not overwhelmed by it, but has dominion over it.'

For Storr, then, creativity may be the outlet by which creative people maintain their sanity, rather than insanity being the force which propels them into orgies of creation. Indeed, it appears that when creative people succumb to mental illness their times of creation are past. Storr gives the examples of Schumann, whose periods of depression prevented him from working, and of Rossini, who suffered equally disabling bouts of illness, even to the point of contemplating suicide. Isaac Newton also suffered from mental illness, but it appears that his attack came on after he had done his major work, although he was still productive.

Others have been even more sceptical about a link. Paul Kline and Colin Cooper set out to test the relationship between psychoticism and creativity first suggested by the Eysencks. They tested over 170 college students for both creativity and psychotic tendencies. They found that the two did not go together: 'These results, on a large sample and with tests that are valid within it, throw some doubt on the generality of the claim made by Eysenck and Eysenck.'

Albert Rothenberg and Paul Burkhardt have looked at the speed with which depressive and schizophrenic patients would respond to a test of word association. In these tests, the subject is given a word and asked to reply with the first word which comes to mind. Slow verbal response is characteristic of depression. So if there were similarities between the psyches of the mentally ill and the creative, you would expect to find that creative people also take longer to reply. Rothenberg and Burkhardt's creative group contained twelve Nobel laureates in the physical sciences. They found that the creative group responded significantly faster than the mentally ill. As they point out, though, a Nobel Prize is enough to ensure social elevation and fame: it might be a little surprising if such people did succumb to depression.

Madness, then, seems to play little role in creativity except to inhibit it. But Anthony Storr's view that creativity is an adaptation that allows people to avoid insanity has a persuasive ring to it.

Divergers and convergers

We probably all hold these two stereotypes in our minds. The first depicts bright, open, intuitive, flexible individuals. They are likely to be the ones who have the ideas, who are always trying something new. They are, in the jargon, divergent thinkers. The other stereotype is of dull, closed-minded, logical and rigid personalities. They do not have ideas of their own. They follow the same well-worn path they have always followed in everything they do. They are the convergent thinkers. It will come as no surprise to learn that some have theorized that these two modes of thinking lie at the root of creativity. Obviously, the divergers are creative, the convergers are not.

Not so obviously.

Divergent and convergent thinking styles were brought to prominence by J. P. Guilford in the 1950s. Guilford was engaged in trying to identify personality traits that seem to be common and important to creative activity. Among others, he suggested that creative people needed *fluency*, associational, expressional and ideational. Associational fluency is shown by the ability to produce a large number of synonyms for a given word in a restricted time. Expressional fluency is measured by asking the subject to make up sentences – the ability to move words around to produce the sentence is apparently connected with creative ability. Ideational fluency is fluency in the production of ideas.

Guilford identified a number of factors that seemed to be important. They included flexibility of thinking, the ability to redefine a problem, aesthetic appreciation, and a tolerance of ambiguity. From them he built up the concept of divergers and convergers. In 'Traits of Creativity' Guilford writes:

> Convergent thinking proceeds towards a restricted answer or solution. If asked 'What is the opposite of high?' you would probably respond with 'Low'. This is an example of convergent thinking. If asked: 'What is two times five plus four?' you would have no other alternative than to say 'Fourteen'. But if you were asked to give a number of words that mean about the same as 'low', you could produce several different responses, all satisfying the requirement, such as 'depressed', 'cheap', 'degraded', and the like, and you would be correct. In this example we have an instance of divergent thinking.

> (quoted in *Creativity* ed. Peter Vernon)

Divergent thinking was seen as a means of improving creativity. If only the bonds of convergence could be loosened, and the diverger in all of us set free, then who knows what we might produce? The idea led directly to the notion of 'brainstorming', developed initially in advertising agencies. Here the 'creative staff' gather to throw ideas at each other. It is hoped that by removing any rules of logic or appropriateness, then something new, original, and valuable will emerge. The evidence that it does so is lacking. That debunker of creativity myths Robert Weisberg has, for instance, reviewed the research into the value of brainstorming in his book *Creativity: Genius and Other Myths*. He concludes: 'Evidence strongly contradicts the claim that withholding judgement is important for creative thinking, and in fact supports the opposite. In other words, the more one knows about the criteria a solution must meet, and the greater role these criteria play in the actual generation of solutions, the better the solution will be.'

Brainstorming, though, does still have its champions, those who believe that modifications to the traditional 'fifteen crazy admen in a box' way of generating ideas can have some value. We will be looking in more detail at how brainstorming might be made to work in Chapter 7.

Liam Hudson also has his doubts about the distinction between convergers and divergers. In his chapter 'The Question of Creativity' in *Contrary Imaginations* he considers two investigations into the prevalence of particular thinking styles in particular pursuits. In the 1950s, Anne Roe studied a group of eminent physical scientists. She found that they had the attributes of the converger. In the 1960s, D. W. MacKinnon carried out a similar study, but included architects and writers as well. He found that creative people tend to think more divergently. In *Contrary Imaginations*, Liam Hudson can find only one way to reconcile these two apparently opposing findings: 'One can only make sense of this evidence . . . by assuming an intellectual spectrum in which each occupation (littérateur, historian, psychologist, biologist, physicist and so on) attracts individuals of a particular personal type. The convergers are naturally attracted towards one end of the spectrum, and the divergers to the other.'

Here is a puzzle. Could someone who is creative in one particular field be equally productive in another, completely separate field? Catch a great writer early enough and could you make instead a great scientist? At the moment we do not know.

Others have embroidered the notion of thinking styles. Perhaps the most famous embellishment is Edward de Bono's 'lateral thinking'. Lateral thinking is designed as an aid to creativity. It is based upon freeing the divergent thinking abilities supposedly nascent inside us all. For de Bono, the way to avoid the problems posed by the spontaneous generation of ideas is to sidestep them. He argues that there is no logical way to explain how hypotheses come into being. There must therefore be another way, the key to which, he suggests, is *provocation*.

He identifies two stages in the thinking process. In the first, we perceive the world around us. In the second we process the impressions and concepts we have observed and defined. Logic is of little use in the first stage, since it has nothing upon which to operate. So to hone this first stage, to make it more productive of ideas, needs some system other than logic. Lateral thinking is such a system. It works by discarding usual methods of thinking based upon judgement, and encouraging the mind to rove wild. To do so, de Bono recommends the use of some provocative stimulus, something that will jolt us out of our usual thinking strategies and into a realm where new patterns, combinations and juxtapositions can occur. In *The Oxford Companion to the Mind*, he gives the example of looking for a new idea for a cigarette product. Pick a word at random. The word turns out to be soap. Soap conjures up thoughts of freshness, of spring, and of putting flower seeds in the butts of cigarettes so that when they are thrown away flowers will grow. As de Bono says, it is hard to see such an idea arising from a conventional, logical analysis of a cigarette.

Lateral thinking has achieved a certain popularity. Magazine articles abound. The government and education authorities in Venezuela are introducing a system in which every schoolchild is led down the path of lateral thinking. They hope thereby to improve the thinking skills of the population.

One test of the worth of lateral thinking will be if we see in twenty years' time an explosion of creative Venezuelans.

There is, though, little evidence to show that lateral thinking is particularly effective, either as a way of explaining how new ideas come into being, or as a way of nurturing creativity. Indeed, it may suffer from the same defects as other forms of brainstorming.

Bending with the breeze

One of the characteristics of divergent thinkers has received particular attention in its own right – flexibility. The argument is simple, and is as follows. To be creative implies the production of new ideas, ideas that haven't occurred to you, or to anyone else, before. To have new ideas means being able to escape from your old ones. Only people with flexibility can do this.

In 1985, Paul Kline and Colin Cooper carried out a study to see if flexibility, and its converse, rigidity, had any strong connection with creativity. They gave undergraduates a battery of psychological tests – including the delightfully named 'balanced dogmatism' test – designed to measure both creative ability and flexibility of thinking. They found that rigid thinking was not the product of a rigid personality. So much for that one.

Many faces

One of the most promising routes into the creative mind is that developed recently by Robert Sternberg.

Sternberg believes that creativity has three faces. In his paper 'A Three Faceted Model of Creativity' he argues that it occurs at 'the peculiar intersection between three psychological attributes: intelligence, cognitive style, and personality/motivation'.

He started by trying to define the qualities of a creative person. He sent out questionnaires to both academics and the general public asking them to indicate which of a set of over 100 personality attributes they most closely associated with creativity. Six major areas emerged. Creative people appeared to be unconventional. They appeared to have the ability to make connections between widely separated ideas. They had taste and imagination. They were able to make decisions, but they had sufficient flexibility to abandon blind alleys. They did not follow received wisdom blindly. They were highly motivated – for whatever reason. Some of these attributes were also present in people's appreciation of what makes a wise person, or an intelligent one, but there was by no means complete overlap. Sternberg points out that any theory of creativity will need to account for this perception of its nature.

One of the keys for Sternberg is his own, earlier, theory of insight. Insight is also three-faceted. In the first stage, selective encoding, the relevant is sifted from the irrelevant in so far as it refers to the problem at hand. Sternberg gives the example of the detective who recognizes the important clues from the unimportant, or of the doctor with a nose for the relevant symptoms leading to a correct diagnosis.

In the second stage, selective combination, individual items of information are assembled into a coherent whole. Sternberg again gives the example of the detective, who, once he has decided which clues to use and which to discard, must then put them together to solve the crime. Another example would be Charles Darwin's production of the theory of evolution. All the information needed to generate that theory had been available for many years before Darwin came upon the problem. His contribution was to synthesize a new way of looking at the world from existing information.

The third stage is selective comparison. Here, new ideas are compared with existing ones. Problem-solving by analogy, suggests Sternberg, involves selective comparison. The power of the analogy is to bring out the realization that the problem being confronted has similarities to some other problem which has already been solved. Shades of associationism!

Sternberg brings his theory to bear by arguing that the 'first facet of creativity is in the application of intelligence in a creative – statistically unusual and highly appropriate – way'. The second facet 'derives from the manner, or style, with which one directs one's intelligence'. And the third is to be found in the personality.

The first facet itself has several aspects. Creative individuals need to bring their intelligence to bear on recognizing the problem to be solved; defining it, and perhaps redefining it into a form which is more easily soluble; considering which of the many methods of solution available is the best. In other words they need insight, operating in the manner Sternberg has suggested.

The second phase – styles of thinking – has to do with the mental habits adopted by people. In particular, Sternberg says that appropriate style – what he calls the legislative style – is found in people who 'a) like to create their own rules, b) like to do things their own way, c) prefer problems that are not prestructured or prefabricated, d) like to build structure as well as content, e) prefer kinds of activities that involve legislation, such as writing papers, designing projects, and creating new business or educational systems, and f) gravitate toward legislative occupations such as creative writer, scientist, artist, sculptor, investment banker, policy-maker or architect.'

None of these would do any good, though, unless something made you get up in the morning. Here is where the third facet becomes essential. There are many aspects to personality that are important here. Creative people must, for instance, not worry about ambiguity. They must be willing to let ideas develop over a period, rather than expecting them to spring fully formed from some fountain. They must be prepared to overcome the obstacles that confront them. They must have perseverance and stamina. They must be able to evaluate the risks inherent in the problems they choose to pursue. It is no good wasting time on something that is insoluble. They must be willing to work for, and wish to attain, some sort of public recognition.

But one of the strongest motivators is the internal drive to create. It appears that those who are driven from outside are less creative than those who motivate themselves. Perhaps the notion of the artist in his garret, driven by inner compulsions, has some truth in it after all.

Sternberg's theory is comprehensive. It is also complex, and draws from many of the other theories so far discussed. Its greatest merit though is that it recognizes that any attempt to explain creativity cannot exist in a vacuum. It can be argued that creativity can be defined in large measure by what we believe it to be, creative people by whom we believe them to be. Sternberg's theory is based firmly on a common-sense view of the nature of creativity, rather than some abstract concept of what it might be.

Two faces in one place – 'Janusian' and 'homospatial' thinking

The American psychiatrist Dr Albert Rothenberg has been involved for some years in attempting to unravel the *process* that goes on during creativity. He had observed that a great deal of previous research on creativity failed to do justice to one essential element – newness. Existing theories tended to be built on the product of creation – the novel, the poem, the scientific discovery. Typically a theorist would then look at the lives of the creative individuals, and try to make connections between events in their lives, and features of their work. If those connections could be made then we would know better what creativity is all about.

Dr Rothenberg believes that this approach produces misleading results. In particular it places too much emphasis on conflicts or problems in the lives of creative people. As he says: 'There is no reason conceptually to believe that because a writer writes about madness, that he or she is mad.'

Dr Rothenberg's view is that it is difficult – if not impossible – to explain newness by invoking the influence of factors that are already in existence – life events, for instance. He therefore set out to study creative work-in-progress. In a series of several thousand interviews he observed creative people in action. His subjects were creative by any definition, Nobel laureates, Pulitzer Prize-winning writers and the like. By following their day-to-day activities, Dr Rothenberg has identified two thinking processes which he believes underlie creativity.

The first is 'Janusian' thinking. The Roman god Janus was possessed of more than one face, each pointing in a different direction. He could therefore perceive a number of different views of the world at the same time. For Rothenberg, one of the essentials of creativity is an ability to hold two opposing ideas simultaneously, and to acknowledge that both of them can be valid or true. He cites as an example the experience of Albert Einstein when he was working on extending his special theory of relativity to include the effects of gravity. The major step was when he suddenly realized that a person could be falling *and* at rest at the same time. 'For an observer in free fall from the roof of a house there exists, during his fall, no gravitational field . . . the observer is therefore justified in considering his state as one of "rest".'

The second thought process Rothenberg calls 'homospatial' thinking. As the name suggests, it involves the ability to hold two or more separate entities within ιe same mental space. Rothenberg suggests that homospatial thinking is particularly vital in the creation of metaphor. Part of the essence of a metaphor is that it lets us see something unfamiliar as being connected with something we know and understand, such as describing the moon as a 'mirror' or a loved one's eyes as gems. Homospatial thinking, like a freshly-minted metaphor, facilitates the bringing together of previously unconnected ideas, concepts or even physical objects, to produce new and striking arrangements.

Albert Rothenberg's theory is one of the few that has been subjected to experimental study. He has tested his ideas by using a form of the word association test described earlier in connection with the creativity and madness investigation. It turns out that creative people do appear to have the ability to hold different ideas in their minds at the same time, and that, given a word, their tendency is to produce its opposite spontaneously. Even when a similar word might seem more poetic or attractive, creative people cling to their natural homospatial style and repeatedly come up with an opposite or even a discord. Thus they will prefer 'black' or 'immoral' as a pair to 'white' rather than such epithets as 'snowy', 'glacial' or 'pure'.

The creative computer

Some computer scientists involved in the search for machine, or artificial, intelligence assert that everything that goes on in the human brain is the result of following a set of rules. This set of rules, or algorithm, determines the path we follow when we solve a problem, for instance, or when we recognize a face. On this view, creative behaviour is merely a matter of following the appropriate algorithm. Presumably some of us have it, and some of us don't. This is a rather crude summary of a complex argument: we will have more to say about the creative computer in Chapter 10.

4

SOME VARIETIES OF CREATIVITY:
A Sideways Look

The reasonable man adapts himself to the world; the unreasonable one persists in trying to adapt the world to himself. Therefore all progress depends on the unreasonable man.

George Bernard Shaw: Man and Superman

So far, we have been looking at creativity in a fairly restricted sense – the sort that produces the *Mona Lisa*, or Beethoven's Fifth. But might there be a more commonplace kind? And if so, how widespread is creativity likely to be within the population? The evidence, as we shall see, suggests that, far from being a rare essence permeating the minds of a fortunate few, the capacity for creation may be ubiquitous. That being so, where is it to be found? Can we, for example, extend the term far beyond its normally used limits of art, music, science and the like, to more everyday circumstances where the 'product' may conform to the criteria of skilful, valuable and innovatory but is transient and mundane?

There is a danger, of course, that the idea of creativity can become so elastic that it could stretch around virtually any behaviour you care to mention. Any thought or action could be instantly labelled 'creative' – whereas it is nothing of the kind. On the other hand there is the converse risk of throwing out the baby with the bath water. We should not dismiss as 'uncreative' behaviour that which does not conform to our preconceptions about what creativity is all about. It can and does dwell in some quite surprising habitats.

Edna and Anna

Edna and Anna in many respects have a lot in common. Both are in their mid-thirties, each married with two children, a caring and hardworking husband and, apparently, a lot going for them: a well-paid job, good looks and, to use the cliché, 'everything to live for'. At this point, though, the similarities end. Edna and Anna are profoundly different in their behaviour and attitudes. Edna is thrifty and sensible about money. Not a skinflint, just reasonably cautious, realizing that a bit of basic budgeting is necessary to allow the family to indulge in all its varied activities. Anna is a spender. She has no thought about 'financial planning', sometimes to the point of recklessness. It is not that she revels in luxury, merely that she sees no need to compare prices in the shops when she has enough in her purse to get instantly what she wants.

The two women differ in other ways as well. Anna goes through the usual motions of being a wife and mother but there is something lacking from her life. She never finds time to talk to her teenage sons, just as somehow she never got round to playing with them when they were toddlers. She cooks and cleans and washes for her husband, but again does not build into her daily timetable occasions when they both sit down and exchange news, gossip and confidences. Actually Anna's time seems to slip by. She reads a little light fiction now and then, but that's about all. Contrast this with Edna. She too has her part-time job but it does not stop her from participating in a wide range of activities, both inside and outside the home.

She makes a point of being available to the children when they want to relate their adventures of adolescence. She tries not to be otherwise engaged when her husband gets home from the office, bursting to off-load some of the frustrations of a demanding job. She arranges for them both to play golf or tennis, too. And she is active in local welfare work.

Taken as a whole the lives of Edna and Anna – two fictitious but typical modern women – differ in one central respect. Where Edna is positive, Anna is neutral. Where Edna makes her mind up to do things, planning, avoiding conflict, building for tomorrow as well as today, Anna lets things drift. One woman makes a happy life for herself and those around her. The other is essentially a blinkered recipient of life's high spots and low points. It is tempting to regard Edna as a 'creative' person – creating a marriage, a home, a life – constantly generating new and valuable experience around herself. The 'product' of her creativity is not anything very tangible nor, you might think, very elevated: just the well-being of a small group of normal, happy people living lives that millions of others enjoy. But, by setting out positively to construct and maintain her life-style, Edna displays a high level of social and emotional engineering skill and, by being flexible in her response to everyday demands and pressures, an admirable level of innovation.

There are, though, limits to this variety of creativity. When Steven and Ethel finally decided to part company after eighteen years of married life, they did so in a sensible and caring fashion. There was no quibbling over sharing the matrimonial home and assets; they showed thoughtfulness and consideration in breaking the news to and maintaining relationships with in-laws and friends. In short, Steven and Ethel's was a civilized divorce, such as might happen quite rarely. Would it justify the description 'creative' though? There may have been skill and novelty in how they set about their break-up. But creativity? Every time we come across sensitivity, tact or intelligence in handling interpersonal relationships – encouraging, even inspiring though this may be – we should not be too indiscriminate in attaching labels. Creative divorce? Creative marriage? Even creative committee chairpersonship? The list of candidates is nigh on endless. But, in reality, the qualifiers are few.

Creating a career

The majority of creative acts are built on what already exists. The great theoretical physicist Richard Feynman once ruefully quoted a remark made to him by a poet. The writer suggested that theoretical physics – even at a Nobel Prize-winning level – was a lot easier to practise than poetry because it consists merely of describing what is already there. Poets have to create their world from nothing.

Not only was the poet undervaluing the immense difficulties of understanding nuclear physics and what might be going on within the confines of the atom, he was also wrong about his own profession. Poets do work with what is already there as well. They have experiences to which to react; emotions and thoughts that need to be given verbal form. True, choosing the right words is not easy, any more than is developing a theory such as quantum electrodynamics or 'superstrings'. It is hard work. But art, like science, steps off from the here and now. What of those who attempt to create something from a world that does not yet and may not ever exist? Such a person is the creative career planner.

In twenty or thirty years' time, it is estimated that half of all the types of jobs that now exist will have disappeared completely. Already we have seen the accelerating trend, away from heavy industry to light, from a manufacturing to a service-based economy, from manual jobs to computerized and soon robotized labour. The pattern will continue. The swallowed-up occupations will be replaced by new ones, while the total knowledge that the human race now possesses will be but a small fraction of what will be available in just a few decades.

This means that anyone just entering the job market, and perhaps intending to stay active therein for thirty or forty years, will have to cope with an enormous amount of change. Gone are the days of being 'in a rut' because the ruts will simply be ironed out by technology or economic necessity. Gone, too, are the days when knowledge and skills acquired now will continue to be marketable several decades in the future. They will not. In fact the successful job holders will be those who have the flexibility of mind and tolerance of uncertainty to cope with novel situations. Career planning becomes less a question of setting your sights on fixed goals than changing your goals to suit your purposes.

If you cannot know or even estimate what will happen you have to be ready for any contingency. This will spell disaster for those who resist novelty or who are sceptical of change, preferring the good old days and the good old ways of doing things. When conventional practices are being overturned it is the improviser, quick on his or her feet and adaptable in outlook, who will survive. Many a future career will be engineered by combining interests or aptitudes not, as is the case with the traditional occupations, in sticking to specialisms. We have already seen this in action in such jobs as computer graphics or medical accounting. What other novel combinations might the year 2000 bring? Veterinary psychologist? Robot personnel officer?

As society changes ever more rapidly it will place a premium on people who are able to juxtapose unlikely concepts; to imagine possible scenarios; to speculate on how things might work better. In short, it will value genuine creators, comfortable to let their minds roam free. If you want to know how you might fit into this scheme of things you can test your futurological skills in the two games below which allow you to predict possible situations involving yourself and other people.

Creative futures: test yourself

We are now in the future. This apparently absurd game is based on our abilities, desires and plans, so try to imagine what else might happen and what external influences, chance situations and possibilities might affect us. With just a little imagination, you can write your memoirs.

1 · Describe your professional situation in 1985.

2 · Describe your personal situation in 1988.

3 · Describe your holiday travel in 1990.

4 · Describe your interests, desires and aspirations in 1992.

5 · Describe your home in 1995.

6 · Describe what you think your place of work will be like in 1999.

7 · Describe a party with friends in 2001.

8 · Describe a weekend in 2003.

9 · Describe your house in 2007.

10 · Describe your personal experiences in 2010.

11 · Describe what you do in your spare time in 2012.

12 · Describe your memories in 2015.

This game is an invitation to play around with what might happen in the future, something like a juggler throwing balls in the air. First of all, choose an area that interests you in terms of your future: Do you want to learn about your job prospects or your domestic arrangements? Describe the situation you are starting with. What could change in the immediate future? What depends on you; on external circumstances? Make brief notes about the consequences, then repeat the process for the period immediately following. The table below gives an example of Mr/Mrs X's chances of success in their friendships.

Initial situation	What happens in the 1st year	Consequences	What happens in the 2nd year	Consequences
	The friend wants to get married.	Look for another friend.		
			Don't find one.	Continue looking.
Mr X has a female friend or Mrs X has a male friend.	The friend gets married to someone you know.	Look for another friend.		
	The friendship doesn't change.	Intensify the friendship.		

Source: Nicola de Carlo, *Psychological Games*, Facts on File Inc., 1984.

Creativity and humour

Humour and creativity have a lot in common. Just as creativity of the kind displayed by our hypothetical Edna is very useful in everyday life, so too is an ability to make jokes. As the British psychologist Dr Hugh Foot puts it:

> There are few more useful social skills than humour. Indeed there are scarcely any social situations in which it is not appropriate even in the direst of plights. Throughout history the most frequently remembered and oft-quoted last remarks of men waiting to be led to the gallows are their rueful witticisms about their fate, society, mankind or life after death.

Remember the deathless line offered by W. C. Fields, for example, when asked to write his own epitaph: 'On the whole I'd rather be in Philadelphia.' Humour in this context becomes a useful means of coping with life's slings and arrows. It can also be used to entertain; to break the ice; to express liking and love; to mediate hostility or contempt; to ingratiate; to control; to lessen tension and anxiety. Laughter offers us an escape from the mundaneness of our daily existence. Humour, as Harvey Mindess says in his book *Laughter and Liberation*, 'offers us release from our stabilizing systems, escape from our self-imposed prisons. Every instance of laughter is an instance of liberation from our controls.'

Any creative piece of work, be it a painting or an invention or a dress design, has a similar effect. It drags us out of what has become conventional or commonplace into a new realm of experience. But the comparison between humour and creativity goes even deeper than this. It lies in the very process itself of making something novel and original. In trying to develop a new work of art or a scientific theory the creative individual has in some measure to escape from the restrictions of convention, fashion or unthinking imitation of others. To make a successful joke one has to fashion from existing materials – words and situations – a novel 'twist' or viewpoint.

There are various ways of doing this. In his perceptive analysis of the process of joke-making, Dr Frank Wicker talks about 'stretching' the meanings of old symbols to create new ones or of 'defrosting' frozen metaphors by reminding us of literal meanings that have nearly disappeared. Consider, he suggests, this example of a defrosted metaphor:

Tarzan came home in the afternoon and asked Jane for a triple bourbon. Jane blurted out, 'Tarzan, I'm worried about your drinking. Every afternoon you come home and get totally sloshed.'

'Jane, I can't help it,' Tarzan protested. 'It's a jungle out there.'

Many jokes, too, depend on irony whereby the meaning of what is being said is precisely the opposite of what the words appear to say. For example:

Question: What is the difference between capitalism and communism?
Answer: Capitalism is the exploitation of man by man. Communism is exactly the opposite.

In both these jokes and in most other kinds of humour, from the subtle ironies, say, of a Jane Austen novel to the pratfall of the red-nosed clown, we laugh in response to a sudden revelation or juxtaposition of meanings or situations. In the Tarzan joke, the word 'jungle' is suddenly transferred to its modern, urban context. In the communism/capitalism story what purports to be a 'difference' looks, at first sight at least, very much like a total similarity. The oldest joke (intentional or otherwise) in the world must be that of the distinguished-looking person, pompous and aloof, suddenly coming down to earth, literally and figuratively, as he slides on a banana skin. Again a rapid juxtaposition that seems incongruous and therefore absurd.

The working methods of the cartoonist Mel Calman who produces incisively amusing drawings for, among others, the London *Times*, show this juxtaposing process in action.

I wrote down a whole lot of words, like . . . let's take rain, for example, 'cos it's always raining in England. And so you're thinking it's wet, you're thinking of duck's feet, you're almost free associating. You're thinking of Noah's Ark, right? And you go through those and you think – well, I did Noah's Ark last time. Is there a fresh way to do Noah's Ark? Is there a fresh way to do webbed feet? And then suddenly while you're doing that, you may think of a total tangential notion of . . . I don't know – something quite different. Or sometimes I just draw two people: a man and a woman, maybe sitting in the rain and then hope that suddenly you'll think of something that one should say to the other which was funny. Or flight delays. There are certain subjects which come round – strikes keep coming round, and each time you think that there must be some new way to think: what's funny about this which I had not thought of before that's fresh? . . . You're making a leap, I think. Humour is making a leap over two seemingly discon- nected things, over which you make a little bridge. And in making the bridge it sometimes is funny. You know, who'd have thought that those two things, instead of being bacon and eggs it's eggs and melon, or something . . . For example, I once had to do a book jacket on noise, and I thought: I cannot think of any way to make a very aural experience into something visual to do with noise. This was a Penguin book – a serious book. And I was stuck in a traffic jam in Oxford Street and there were some men drilling in the road. And I suddenly thought: gosh, that's what it's like – it's like somebody drilling right inside your head. That's what really bad noise is. So then I – which was easy – I found an image. So I could do a drawing of a man drilling inside a head. And then – I was working with another designer – and we got an engraving of the inside of a person's ear. So you got another element. But sometimes you make associations quite suddenly. I think a lot of the time you're brooding away without your knowing you're doing it. I'm not talking about topical work. I'm talking about general things. You suddenly think: Oh well, that's what I was thinking, without realizing that's what I was thinking about, and you've solved it.

What emerges from Mel Calman's insights into his own skilled jokemaking is that having new or absurd or unconventional ideas about a subject is not enough. Nor is it sufficient just to juxtapose these at random. That may be the first step, but thereafter the effective humorist goes on to select those combinations of ideas and fashion them into the sorts of images that will prove most telling. Harvey Mindess, who draws many parallels between the joke and other forms of creativity, sums it up thus: 'Conceived, like its more illustrious relatives, in a burst of inspiration, the humorous product too may be shaped and refined in painstaking dedication.'

Again we have come back to that inescapable combination of inspiration and effort, the sudden insight coupled with the craftsman's skill, that lies at the heart of all creative acts. Both are necessary. A would-be cartoonist for example may be very strong in the purely technical department, having succeeded brilliantly in all his art school examinations for composition and technique. But without novel ideas on which to work, this technique alone will not raise a smile let alone a guffaw among his audience.

What is true of the humble newspaper cartoon of course is also true of the ceiling paintings in the Sistine Chapel or Van Gogh's sunflowers. Technique alone is never enough. Nor is a desire to say something or even having something important to say. There has to be a perfectly balanced fusion of the two. In the well-turned joke we instantly can judge whether the marriage has worked. We laugh. Or not, as the case may be.

One further important comparison between a work of art and a joke – be it verbal or visual – lies in their ability to give us insights into our own characters and personalities. Jokes come in many different varieties: sick or healthy; cruel or kind; racist or liberal; 'dirty' or 'clean' to mention but a handful of categories. Not everyone likes all kinds of humour. We have preferences and dislikes determined by what we are as thinking, feeling beings. Consider these two jokes for example:

> *Patient*: Doctor, doctor, everyone keeps ignoring me.
> *Doctor*: Next patient please!

Or:

> A married couple are walking through the zoo when a gorilla leaps out and attempts to have sexual intercourse with the woman. 'Help,' she yells, 'this ape's trying to rape me.' The husband smiles wryly and says, 'Well, why not tell it you've got a headache?'

Now to many if not most people these are fairly harmless jokes. Whether or not you find them particularly funny is a matter of taste. But some people might find them decidedly unfunny. A person suffering from genuine feelings of loneliness or alienation, to the point where these are beginning to become a psychiatric problem, might wince at the doctor–patient exchange. It would simply be too close to the psyche for comfort. Similarly a man or woman experiencing severe marital disharmony through sexual incompatibility might well be very distressed indeed to find their dilemma encapsulated in a silly joke about a libidinous gorilla.

We can to some extent, then, explore the kinds of people we are through analysing our reactions to humour of different kinds. We can identify those areas of our life that we might wish to keep hidden and those we are totally frank about. We can use humour, too, as a barometer of our attitudes and prejudices, and through this learn more about ourselves. This of course is precisely the function of a creative work of art or literature. They, too, stir deep feeling and confront us with ourselves in other guises – 'a mirror up to nature' – sometimes offering consolation and solace when we need it. In fact a joke, like a novel, can be a creative way of analysing our own psyches. Which brings us to another variety of creativity: psychotherapy.

Creativity on the couch

'Poets and psychotherapists are blood brothers . . . both share a vital interest in the understanding and enhancement of the human heart, its emotions and its experiences.' Few people would quarrel with that broad statement. It was made by the psychiatrist Dr Albert Rothenberg, but could well have come from the pen of the founding father of psychoanalysis, Sigmund Freud. Freud, too, drew parallels between the work of writers and painters and that of doctors trying to help patients suffering various emotional upsets or traumas. Indeed it was from Freud's acute fascination with the subtleties of other people's minds, the way in which experiences form behaviour and shape conscious and unconscious feelings, that Freudian psychoanalytic theory and practice were born. The influence of Freud on subsequent generations of therapists has been incalculable, both in shaping their methods of intervention and in deepening their understanding of 'the human heart'. To underscore the similarity between poets and psychotherapists to which Albert Rothenberg refers, much of Freud's writing is itself highly poetic in character, charged with metaphors and similes, colourful and imaginative in its reconstruction in words of what might be going on in the shady recesses of the id or the ego.

This much is self-evident from glancing at Freud's books such as *The Interpretation of Dreams*, or simply by thinking about the day-to-day work of an analyst as he patiently listens to a client's revelations about his early life or his current fears and phobias. Truly poetry and psychotherapy tread common ground. What is less obvious to the outsider is the striking similarity uncovered by Albert Rothenberg in his extensive research between the actual process of writing a poem and the clinical methods of the therapist.

Dr Rothenberg is an investigator we have already encountered in Chapter 6 where we saw him attempting to unravel what many tend to regard as an inscrutable mystery. For the moment, though, let us stay with him in his capacity as a practising psychoanalyst interested in how his own professional techniques compare to those of the working poet.

First of all he had to build up a data base on how poems are made. He did this by talking at length and in depth to leading American poets, winners of Pulitzer Prizes, the Bollingen Poetry Award or the National Book Award, and often members of the American Academy of Arts and Letters. He watched poems in the making, from the first few words and lines to the finished piece, talking regularly to their creators in order to tease out what was going on during the constructional process. Next he analysed his own work as a therapist and that of other practitioners to see what, if any, were the broad areas of similarity.

He found that poetic creation and psychotherapy share certain essential features, in process as well as content. They have a beginning and an end point; they both emphasize verbal communication as the primary means of interaction; and usually, but not invariably, both have the goal of achieving psychological insight.

The starting-point for a poem, often termed its 'inspiration', does not as it turns out conform to the popular image of a sudden surge of dramatic feelings and images in the poet's head. In fact the poets that Rothenberg studied rarely reported a sudden inspirational experience at the beginning of the poem. Indeed they had few such experiences at any time during the course of creation. 'True creators,' he says, 'are primarily those people who can work out ideas of any sort, inspired or uninspired.'

Nevertheless there is a definite beginning to the making of a poem, characterized by some degree of impulse to do something, to write down, often just in jotted note form, a few words; or it may simply take the form of an active resolution in the mind to remember words that have come into one's head and write them down at a convenient time later on. Step one, then, is that of tension, an urge to get down to work and start writing. This initial tension is quite specific: 'It is . . . an anxiety about finding out what the poem is really about.' Over and over again Rothenberg's subjects told him that they seldom knew what message their poems contained until they had actually finished them. At that point the tension dissolves into feelings of illumination, discovery and often considerable relief.

Now compare this form of creative beginning and ending to what goes on in psychotherapy. The initial idea for a poem might be compared to a patient's symptoms. Here too there is tension, deriving often from deep-seated conflicts that, once resolved, bring relief. The therapist helps to bring these conflicts and anxieties into the open. Sometimes, when he does, the patient finds new symptoms to trouble him while learning perhaps to live with the old ones. Or he might achieve a degree of self-insight that obliterates the symptoms altogether.

Roughly speaking, this process, argues Rothenberg, follows that of poetic creation. The poet's initial drive or impulse approximates to the emotionally troubled person's symptoms. Both call for resolution. The poet, like the therapist, works on an initial idea to modify it, in the process reducing tension and building to a state of eventual relief. At that point both poet and therapist, together with patient, have acquired a deeper sense of self-awareness or insight.

But there are even more significant similarities, what Dr Rothenberg calls the meeting place of 'psychological freedom'. The poet decides when his poem is finished, just as the patient decides that he has had enough treatment. That is the free choice both make. In addition, if psychotherapy has been effective the patient 'comes to feel free of the enslaving and distorting effect of his past', he or she throws off the conflicts or attitudes that have been creating a psychological prison. This means that successful therapy ends when the patient 'has arrived at or come close to his maximum of psychological freedom and uniqueness'. So, too, with a poem. This is also a move towards psychological freedom. The poet is often motivated by ideas that are metaphorical expressions of personal conflicts. Because making the poem will involve him in working through these conflicts and achieving insight, the poet usually feels liberated from the past. And, as with good psychotherapy, this freeing of the individual produces an improvement in psychological functioning. It is therapeutic.

The singer and the song

Another variety of creativity is *re*-creativity. An actor takes a part that has been played many times before and makes of it something new, valuable and original. A musician or conductor picks up a score interpreted by hundreds of others and manages to bring to it something exciting, as if it were being heard for the very first time. In cases like these it is difficult not to acknowledge that the interpreter is a creator as well. Although using another piece of work as a source without which there would be no performance, he or she is not simply voicing the words or playing the notes in a passive fashion. There is nothing automatic or stereotyped about an expressive interpretation. It requires and demands an enormous amount of effort, first to uncover a meaning or a message, then, second, to express this in a distinctive way for an audience.

In a sense, one might almost say that a play or a concerto are 'finished' by a fine interpretation. The work of art may be an acknowledged masterpiece in its own right, yet it may still be enhanced in performance. The interpreter and the originator – often with centuries separating their lives – join forces to produce a total creation. The two acquire a joint identity. Thus we might talk about 'Leonard Bernstein's Stravinsky' or 'Laurence Olivier's Hamlet' to reflect how the original changes according to who is interpreting it.

Once again we can, in some degree, apply this variety of creativity more widely than is commonly supposed. We probably all have a recollection of at least one good teacher, at school or college; someone who purveyed knowledge in a stimulating, entertaining or inspiring fashion, someone, perhaps, who set us on a particular path that determined the rest of our lives. Here again is an individual who acts positively on a given body of knowledge and manages to endow it with a more attractive quality than the teacher who drily and unimaginatively serves up the facts parrot-fashion. The contrast can be quite staggering. One history teacher for example will, with scrupulous care and attention to detail, ensure that his students are given all the dates and events they need to answer an examination question. Another will make ostensibly remote happenings completely relevant to the modern world, will give shape to the course of history and breathe life into its characters. The first teaches history. The second imparts a sense of history. Both are interpreting the same data base.

A common thread: problem-solving

What, if anything, is common to all these varieties of creativity? We have seen that all have elements of novelty, originality or value. Is there anything else that links activities as disparate as composing a piano sonata or running a household, making up a joke and carving out a career?

Many researchers into the creative process tend to the view that a common denominator is that of problem-solving. The creative person is one who is adept at finding solutions to problems. Now here, of course, the word 'problem' itself begs many questions. Problems are what we have to wrestle with during school physics lessons; they are the sorts of topics discussed by anxious people considering the pros and cons of having Granny to live in or letting the teenage daughter go out with an older man. Problems are difficult matters that we have to struggle with in order to find the best outcome – namely, the solution. This can be as unitary as the bottom line of a page of algebra or as messy as the either/or, ifs and buts conclusions we arrive at in our everyday social or family life.

Where does creativity fit into the scheme of things? So far as science is concerned, it is easy to make the connection between, say, an imaginative and useful theory and problem-solving because such a theory does indeed represent a solution to a problem: that of explaining some data or phenomena. Thus, when faced with the fact that male birds have more ostentatious plumage than females or that some city-dwelling moths tend to be dark in colour, we can explain both by recourse to Darwin's theory of natural selection. The theory tells us why these phenomena exist. It is because they are adaptive. A dull male would not win many mates nor deter many competitors. A brightly conspicuous moth would easily be picked off by a predator against the dull background of a cityscape. The problem is to explain. The solution is the explanation.

When we come to consider the 'problem-solving' activities of other creative individuals the link is, at first sight at least, less clear. Surely poets, novelists, painters, sculptors, musicians and the like are in the business of self-expression, not solving problems as such? This view of artistic creation is understandable but, in the opinion of Dr Robert Weisberg, too narrow. Dr Weisberg contends that the thought processes involved when scientists solve important problems are precisely the same as those of the creative artist. Indeed, he goes further and suggests that both share those same thinking processes with ordinary people solving simple everyday problems. We shall return to this suggestion a little later, but for the present let us stay with the arts/sciences connection. The artist, says Dr Weisberg, is not someone who, out of the blue, suddenly brings works into being: 'individual works of art,' he writes, 'do not spring full-blown into the artist's head, but evolve as he or she attempts to deal with "problems" in the early versions of the work.'

To illustrate this contention he points to the career of the celebrated American sculptor Alexander Calder (1898–

1976) who is credited with giving the world a new art form: the mobile. Before Calder there were no hanging constructions in offices, shops and homes – including the toys swinging above the baby's crib. Before Calder no one had incorporated the breeze-induced movement of shapes into their work so that constantly changing spaces and geometries become part of the means of expression. It seems as if around the autumn of 1931 the mobile sprang into being from nowhere. But this was not the case.

In fact, as Dr Weisberg stresses, there were a number of clearly identifiable influences on Calder in the preparatory years before 1931. The artist did not make huge intuitive leaps, but approached his art from what one might almost call an 'engineering' standpoint. How to make sculptures from hand-made pieces? How to arrange for them to move? How to extend the techniques Calder had already used for making action toys to more abstract shapes and forms? How to take in the powerful influence of the abstract painter Mondrian and so on? At all stages Calder set himself practical tasks. 'Indeed,' concludes Dr Weisberg, 'it might not be too far-fetched to say that Calder's career involved a long-term exercise in problem-solving: How could he apply his particular skills and interests to as wide a range of phenomena as possible?'

When one contemplates other artistically creative people at work, what was true of Calder begins to look as if it may be applicable more generally. Artists themselves may sometimes talk glibly or mysteriously about an idea or a phrase 'just coming out of the blue' – like Samuel Taylor Coleridge and his poem *Kubla Khan*. In reality they have to work hard on a number of drafts or sketches to get them right. As we have seen, this is true even of Coleridge's poem. The famous published version was in fact preceded by a draft. It did not come out of nowhere.

More often creative people working in the arts describe their efforts to create not in grandiose inspirational terms but as a way of resolving technical problems, of taking existing materials or formulae and reworking them until something innovatory emerges. They talk about developing an idea by constant revisions and excisions. They talk of trying to achieve freedom of expression within a given framework. This means familiarizing themselves with their materials, constantly experimenting with new ways of exploiting them. This seems to be the outlook and strategy of the actor-writer-director and Renaissance man of the theatre, Jonathan Miller, whose ideas we shall be exploring in greater depth in the next chapter.

Perhaps the supreme example of the artist as problem-solver is the composer J. S. Bach. Bach worked at a period when rules of musical composition were quite rigid. There were specified ways of writing fugues or setting words to music of a religious nature. The composer had no freedom to establish his own guidelines – as is the case nowadays, say, with contemporary music – but had to accept the conventions of his day. The tools of his trade and the materials he could use were handed to him off the shelf. Indeed, in the case of Bach and his contemporaries, it was quite commonplace as well to borrow ideas from other composers. The music of Vivaldi figures quite prominently in Bach's output, albeit in an altered form.

Here then was Bach's problem: to produce a cantata or a concerto employing extremely well-used compositional rules and strategies without making them sound like formula music, a kind of aural painting by numbers. That he succeeded in doing so is indicative of the very special gifts of Bach compared to lesser composers of the day who were drawing on exactly the same toolkit. But these gifts are in part those of the practical problem-solver. The 'genius' component only accounts for some of Bach's unique music. In fact one might argue that it accounts for hardly any of it, perhaps even none at all.

Someone who would agree with that notion is the contemporary British designer Sir Terence Conran, the founder of the prodigiously successful Habitat chain of retail shops and subsequently the head of a massive empire of retail outlets worldwide. Conran firmly believes that design is in a great degree problem-solving, especially when aimed at a mass market. 'You're dealing,' he says, 'with a market where price is a constraint, you're trying always to squeeze a quart from a pint pot. You know ideally what you would like to achieve, and you have so many restrictions of costs and marketing that, in order to achieve this, you have to work very carefully.'

Terence Conran also stresses that he sees a good deal of common ground between the two sides of his own work – as a designer and as a businessman. Both are founded on common sense. Just as the industrialist or banker has to sort out his marketing, his cash flow, his financing, so too does the designer. The example he cites is Brunel, a brilliant engineer who had to sell his innovative ideas to railway and shipping companies and then control the costing and scheduling of their production. In the same league were the brothers Michelin who not only designed tyres but then thought up creative ways of marketing them, through publishing guides and maps, holding race meetings and touring events, and even making road signs. 'They were using creativity in the widest sense of the word to see that the smallish product they had made actually inspired the world.'

Problem-solving, in whatever field, is often a matter of perspective, of seeing the problem from the right angle. This is true of the artist and scientist, as well as in more everyday circumstances. By altering your angle of vision or, as Dr Edward de Bono might put it, by contemplating a variety of 'information universes' you can often gain valuable insight.

Consider for example this problem set by Dr de Bono in an article on 'The Future of Thinking'.

Three people are holding similar blocks of wood. One releases his block and it falls to the ground. Another lets go of his piece and it moves upwards. The third lets go and the block stays exactly where it is. Explain these three different behaviours. You cannot do so if you persist in thinking that all three blocks of wood exist in the same 'universe': if they did their behaviour would be identical. Think instead of alternative universes. In fact, person number two is under water – hence the block floats upwards. Person number three is orbiting the earth in a space vehicle where zero gravity ensures that the block floats where it is. 'The mystery,' writes de Bono, 'is cleared up once we can specify the universe in which the action is taking place.'

It is this ability or drive to seek different universes that generates creativity. In the case of the block problem we are forced to consider alternative scenarios in order to reach the correct answer. In fields where there is no 'right' or 'wrong' but there are still problems to be resolved – as for writers or painters – the individual has to motivate him- or herself to inhabit new universes. The next chapter provides some insights into how 'creative people' achieve this end.

Summary

1 · Creativity can exist in social relationships, even in planning one's life, as well as in art and science.

2 · There are important comparisons to be made between humour and creativity, both in the final product and in the process by which it is achieved.

3 · Similarly, there are interesting parallels between the process of creation and psychotherapy: both are, in a sense, a resolution of an initial state.

4 · The interpreter of a work of art may be as creative as its original maker.

5 · Problem-solving seems to be a common thread running through all forms of creativity.

5

CREATIVE VOICES

The true artist will let his wife starve, his children go barefoot, his mother drudge for his living at seventy, sooner than work at anything but his art.

George Bernard Shaw: Man and Superman, Act I

One way to find out about creativity is the horse's mouth strategy: by asking creative people themselves to talk about how they do it. Unfortunately, the results can be very disappointing. The horse's mouth, to mix a metaphor, has a habit of ejecting a curate's egg. One reason for this, perhaps, is that creative people are primarily good at being creative, not at analysing their own mental processes. Certainly, when you boil down the wise words of great artists and writers and the like, they do tend to amount to little more than unrevealing generalities such as, 'Sometimes I'm in a really productive mood. At other times I'm not.' Or they can sound pretentious, as if the individual, being put on the spot by an interrogator, were concocting something to appear convincing through its sheer verbosity.

On the other hand, some creative people do manage, without self-consciousness or pomposity, to convey something of the process by which they achieve their ends. In a revealing series of interviews a number of well-known creators came up with some genuine insights. They were: Terence Conran, designer, founder of the Habitat chain of furniture, hardware and fabrics shops and subsequently the head of a multi-million pound international retailing organization; the actor/writer/director Dr Jonathan Miller; the brilliantly successful British comedy playwright Michael Frayn; Jean Muir, the dress designer whose clothes are synonymous with elegance and style; Mel Calman the writer and cartoonist whose small, sparsely-drawn characters have given voice to so many commentaries on contemporary life; David Ogilvy, the advertising man whose campaigns have teased money from the pockets of consumers from one corner of the globe to the other. Taken in concert with other creative voices their views add up to an important contribution to our understanding of the creative mind.

To begin with, they were asked whether they were conscious

of being creative, in the sense of pondering on their skill.

Do creative people think about the process of creativity?

Some creative individuals including the novelist William Trevor seem to be ambivalent on this point. On the one hand they seem to prefer to swim in murky waters of artistic accomplishment without knowing where they are going. On the other they are obviously keen to reflect on their lack of orientation. Trevor once stated: 'It is very important for writers of fiction not to know exactly where everything comes from. There is this mysterious area in which we operate. It's a bad thing to analyse it . . . You've got to belong in a sort of fog most of the time, and when you penetrate the fog, everything is clear, you see everything absolutely clearly, especially yourself and your abilities, you are retired or dead!'

Jean Muir certainly thinks a lot about her own creativity: 'Whatever form of design or art it is, it's a continuous process. I'm simultaneously analysing what I've done, what I'm doing at the present and what I need to do . . . those three things constantly move within each other all the time . . . a constant chain of ideas.'

Likewise Mel Calman: 'Well, I think about it a lot because it's mysterious and yet you cannot afford to be too mysterious because you're trying to earn a living at being creative.'

Michael Frayn has a similar view: 'I don't think about creativity as an abstract subject, but I do think a great deal about whether I can write or I can't write.' He adds with a smile: 'Sometimes I can. And sometimes I can't!' The message that comes through from most creative people seems to be that they are indeed very conscious of their abilities, obsessed, even, about their functioning whether this be, as in Calman's case, for economic reasons, or for the more abstract satisfaction of seeing a task through to a successful conclusion. But not everyone agrees. Jonathan Miller is quite unequivocal about the futility of creative self-consciousness: 'Almost always when people are self-conscious about creating things it is self-defeating. Nothing comes out of it. If people think of themselves as wanting to be a creative artist they'll never ever be one.' And as Terence Conran points out, thinking about one's creativity is not the same as understanding it: 'It's possible to analyse the creative process up to the moment when it turns from being quite a useful, sensible but dull object into something that really has got a great deal of style, charm, zip and fizz about it . . . Design is 98 per cent common sense and 2 per cent that mystical ingredient that you might call creativity. But it's that thing that makes a perfectly decent object into something really special, really desirable that people want as much as they might want a Picasso on the wall.'

Where do creative ideas come from?

What, then, is that elusive 2 per cent all about? How does a person catch hold of it? Here the opinions of creative individuals seem to be shaped in one direction or the other by the ideas of Sigmund Freud with his predilection for unconscious thought processes: 'A strong experience in the present awakens in the creative writer a memory of an earlier experience (usually belonging to his childhood) from which there now proceeds a wish which finds its fulfilment in the creative work. The work itself exhibits elements of the recent provoking occasion as well as of old memory.' ('Creative writers and daydreaming')

Among Freud's disciples on this score is the adman David Ogilvy: 'Nobody ever arrives at a very big idea through a conscious, rational thought process. It comes from your unconscious.' Not only does Ogilvy subscribe to the unconscious as a source of creative ideas, he also endorses another well-known Freudian notion – that of the power of dreaming to liberate the imagination: 'I was doing a campaign once for a manufacturer, and I couldn't think of an idea, and I was kind of desperate about it. The night before I had to show something to my client I had a dream, an interesting dream. I woke up and for once in my life I wrote it down and went back to sleep. Next morning I went to the office and had that dream out into a TV commercial which is still running thirty years after and which has made that particular product the leader in its field. That's an extreme form of unconscious creation. I didn't think my way to it.'

Michael Frayn shares David Ogilvy's 'out of the blue' perception of creativity: 'Ideas certainly do just come out of nowhere. No doubt some of them come because one has been thinking about a subject, researching it, pursuing it. But in the end, the idea just comes to one from nowhere, or it doesn't, and one has absolutely no control over that whatever.'

Interestingly, sleep, or at least lack of it, has played a part in at least one of Frayn's successful plays: 'The very first television play I wrote was composed completely in my head (which is not the way I normally work) on a night of insomnia. I couldn't sleep. I lay awake all night and saw all the characters and the entire plot. I don't know why, but anyway I wrote the play more or less like I saw it, cut off the first ten minutes which were not necessary, and that was it. If only my other plays would get themselves written like that.'

As Frayn ruefully suggests, the trouble with the unconscious as a hothouse for creative ideas is that it follows its own rules and procedures. It goes its own idiosyncratic way. David Ogilvy, though, believes the power of the unconscious mind can, to some extent, be deliberately harnessed: 'First of all you have to brief your unconscious. Then you have to switch off your thought processes and wait for something, for your unconscious to ring you up and say, "Hey, I've got a

good idea!" There are ways to do that. A lot of people find that
to take a long hot bath produces good ideas. Other people
prefer a long walk. I've always found that wine produces good
ideas – the better the wine the better the idea.'

The more you probe David Ogilvy's method of working in
tandem with his unconscious the more it emerges that
conscious thinking plays more than just a glancing role.
Indeed for Ogilvy there would be no unconscious creativity
without a great deal of conscious problem defining and
focusing: 'I read an awful lot about a particular product and
its consumers and what the public at large thinks of it
and why they use things like that. I've studied the competitive
advertising that's been run for similar products. And I've
found out which of those campaigns was the most successful
in terms of sales. So my unconscious by this time is pretty
well briefed. The rest is prayer.'

In the world of interior design Terence Conran too believes that creativity favours the prepared mind: 'You find out
what people want by observing them: their life-styles; where
they go on holiday; what they read; what music they listen to;
what they eat. You're thinking about their lives. It's often
imagining what they might want before they actually get it.
Sometimes you go too far and it's a commercial flop. It's got
to be one or two steps ahead, not a cricket pitch ahead.'

At the same time, though, Conran believes that sometimes good design emerges from situations where the rules
have been flouted: 'Very often you've heard from your client
the brief, and something happens quickly, and you've got the
idea for it. Now that's the wrong way round, because you
should go through the whole process of study, thought,
looking at various different alternatives until you get to the
end of the road. But often it happens the other way round.
Suddenly as you're listening this idea happens and you know
it's right. Then you have to work backwards to prove it . . .
We try to train designers not to work in this way. We try to

teach them to absorb all the facts before they put pen to paper but . . . I can remember the design for the Citycorp Building actually happening with the architect as he was listening to the brief. His initial back-of-envelope sketch bore some relation to what eventually occurred.'

When do creative ideas emerge?

What many aspiring architects, or indeed anyone else striving for new ideas, would dearly like to know of course is why a particularly successful notion should choose to present itself when it does. In her perceptive book *Notebooks of the Mind*, Vera John-Steiner casts around for an answer by looking at the writings of creators such as the composer Aaron Copland. His view is clear enough: 'You can't pick the moment when you are going to have ideas. It picks you and then you might be completely absorbed in another piece of work.' Later Copland goes on to expand on this theme: 'I think composers will tell you that they get ideas when they can't possibly work on them. They put them down where they can find them when they need to look for ideas and they don't come easily.'

The idea of a creative thought hitting one out of the blue like a random roll of a lucky dice finds an echo in the inventor Steve Temple. He believes that: 'There is an awful lot of serendipity . . . 50 per cent of the ideas are really cross-fertilization of technology due to my working on many and varied projects.'

Jonathan Miller does not like the word 'creativity' at all. He prefers to see himself as a problem-solver. The problems range from broad initial considerations such as 'In what century shall I set this opera?' to the more technical challenges such as 'How do I get the tenor across the stage and into the wings before the music comes to an end?' Miller has found that very often the solutions to his artistic problems arrive at what he calls 'the moment of inadvertence': 'At the moment when you glimpse the problem out of the side of your eye rather than confront it head-on, then it seems to solve itself. Maybe this is because this allows unexpected streams of thought to take over. Maybe when you're concentrating on something and it's right in the centre of your vision you are in some way a victim of conventional styles of thought . . . what you do is let the computer idle, and in those off-guard moments the solution occurs.' He recalls a particular example when he was working with a designer on the set of a new play. They had reached an impasse, totally unable to come up with a solution which would work for the particular production. Then came a moment of inadvertence: 'We were simply sitting talking about other things when out of the corner of my eye I saw the *back* of the model of the set we had used for the previous play. I saw that the back of the model was actually the set that we needed to use as the front for the next production. It's often paying attention to the rubbish on the edge of life that helps to solve problems.'

For Mel Calman, though, the process of idea acquisition is rather different. He subscribes to the 'perspiration not inspiration' school of thought: 'When Raymond Chandler was stuck for ideas he would rent a hotel room with nothing to read. Eventually sheer boredom drove him to work. I think a lot of creative people are like that.' Calman denies the value of 'inspiration': 'Inspiration is not a useful word. It sounds as if Madame Muse might be sitting around somewhere. A better analogy is the radio receiver. I communicate with the unconscious part of myself and when it's going well it's wonderful. When it's not going well it is like a radio crackling with interference.'

In order to establish good idea-reception some creative people look to those who went before them as a source of innovation. Here it seems that precedents can be useful provided they are chosen with care. Hermann Hesse in his

Autobiographical Writings recorded: 'At first, swimming in modern, indeed the most modern literature, and in fact being overwhelmed by it was an almost intoxicating joy . . . after that first joy was exhausted, it became necessary to me to return from my submersion in novelties to what is old.'

As well as trying to discover how people manage to be creative, there is also the question of why they choose to be so. Is creative work driven by a sense of purpose? If so, what is it?

The creative purpose

Many creators would agree with the innovative dramatist Harold Pinter when he declared: 'I write because I want to write' ('Writing for Myself'). The art critic John Berger says something similar in 'Toward Reality': 'Only if we recognize the mortality of art shall we cease to stand in such superstitious awe of it; only then shall we consider art expendable and so have the courage to risk using it for our own immediate, urgent, only important purposes.'

Those purposes according to Terence Conran may be nothing more than the desire to improve one's surroundings: 'I've never met a truly creative person . . . who was happy and satisfied with life. They are always worried about something, that something is not right. They could improve the world. What I was trying to do was say that the way home furnishings were being retailed was bloody awful. I needed through creativity, inspiration . . . whatever . . . and quite a lot of common sense, to find a better way of doing it. To present things in a more stimulating environment.' David Ogilvy, on the other hand, with characteristic no-nonsense candour, looks to finance as his driving force: 'I only started being any good when I was being paid for it. For me, for a lot of people, money is the great spur. It concentrates the mind . . . like hanging.'

Compare this viewpoint with that expressed over and over again by other creators who are essentially driven internally by the excitement of making something. It is common to hear talk of a *desire* or even a *longing* to create and inhabit the world of their imagination. They experience almost a physical pleasure in consummating their art. Jonathan Miller likens his creative activities to a child absorbed in a game: 'A child building a sandcastle is not "working hard". It doesn't seem to him to be a task. It simply fills his imagination at the time it's going on, and anything else is an irritant. I suppose a great deal of expenditure (of energy) is going on, but a child that's playing hard never thinks it's working hard . . . When I'm being productive, I don't think I'm working hard. I simply don't think of anything else.'

Whether ambition or excitement be the driving force behind a work of creation, it is never effortless. Hard work plays a universal part in creativity. David Ogilvy says on this point: 'If you know anything you can do successfully and well without working hard, I wish you'd tell me what it is, and I'll have it for my next job in my next incarnation . . . Work hard at it and don't settle for lousy ideas.' In his discussion of the painter and sculptor Giacometti, Rollo May depicts a man driven daily to start again: 'In order to go on, to hope, to believe that there is some chance of his actually creating what he ideally visualizes, he is obliged to feel that it is necessary to start his entire career over again, every day, as it were from scratch' (*The Courage to Create*).

What makes creative work especially hard, according to the designer and historian Stephen Bayley is its success – or rather failure – rate. 'The capacity to sustain failure is important,' says Bayley whose words accord well with those of Calman: 'I have sat at *The Times*,' says Calman, 'and scribbled and scribbled away and nothing's happened. The only thing that makes me do something is the feeling that it will be worse tomorrow if I went home. It'll be worse tomorrow.'

There is for Mel Calman and, likewise, for Terence Conran no easy path towards a work of genuine creativity. It all takes patience, self-discipline and self-honesty. Conran says: 'You have to take the slings and arrows of life and benefit from them. And be pretty self-critical as well and say to yourself that something wasn't good enough. To see why it got rejected.' Mel Calman would agree: 'I tend to discipline myself because otherwise I wouldn't get any work done. I never wander around waiting for something to happen.'

How important is self-criticism and self-discipline?

'About one and a half manuscript pages constitute my daily stint. This slow method of working springs from severe self-criticism and high requirements in matters of form.' Thus wrote the German novelist Thomas Mann. Likewise Iris Murdoch: 'I live, I *live*, with an absolutely continuous sense of failure. I am always defeated, always. Every book is the wreck of a perfect idea. The years pass and one has only one life. If one has a thing at all one must do it and keep on and on and on trying to do it better' (quoted by Gail Godwin in her essay 'Becoming a Writer').

One route to self-discipline that creative people such as Jean Muir point to as important is the physical limitations of the medium in which they are working: 'I like discipline . . . the innate feeling of being disciplined. It forms a structure within which you can then do what you want. I hate the term "free expression" as a matter of fact. Most people work better within a discipline. Most painters even if they're abstract artists say that their years of life drawing gave them the most extraordinary discipline, a sense of structure, and proportion, balance, shape and movement.'

Are creative people morose and depressed?

Given the undeniable hardships involved in creating something satisfactory, are creative individuals more pessimistic or glum than the rest of us? In his book on Pete Seeger the folk singer David Dunaway argues that the answer to this question is 'Yes'. 'The musician who thrives on poverty and despair has become a cliché; yet in Seeger's case, when everything tipped against him, when his liberty, career, and safety were in jeopardy, a spark inside ignited a song' (*How Can I Keep From Singing: Pete Seeger*). From a broader perspective of studying the psychology of many creative people the psychiatrist Silvano Arieti comes to the same conclusion: 'The creative person . . . feels himself in a state of turmoil, restlessness, deprivation, emptiness, and unbearable frustration unless he expresses his inner life in one or another creative way' (*Creativity: the Magic Synthesis*). In more succinct terms Mel Calman puts it this way: 'I worry a lot.'

For all this apparent psychological turmoil though creative people do genuinely enjoy their work with an almost childlike delight. Witness Michael Frayn: 'When it's going well I've always felt it ridiculous one should be paid money for it. It's so wonderful, so delightful, and such a completely absorbing experience.' Likewise Steve Temple: 'It's a hell of a lot of fun doodling on a white board . . . Tedious? It's sheer excitement!' Dennis Gabor, the inventor of holography, said as much about Einstein in the course of an interview: 'No one has ever enjoyed science as much as Einstein. Scientific problems, you might say, simply melted in his mouth . . . When he spoke of relativity . . . The formulae were no longer abstract, they came to life through Einstein's lectures. One could almost say he did gymnastics while lecturing.' Einstein clearly loved doing science. Harold Pinter has a similar ability to immerse himself in his own activities: 'I did it – and still do it – for my own benefit; and it's purely accident if anyone else happens to participate. Firstly and finally, and all along the line, you write because there's something you *want* to write, *have* to write. For yourself' ('Writing for Myself').

Surprisingly, perhaps, Michael Frayn does not even consider his audience when setting out to craft a play: 'I never think about consumer, reader, or member of the audience when I'm writing. Writing just seems to be a sort of compulsion to develop that particular material – to do what I can with that idea and those people. I can't see any other way to go about it. I can't think to myself 'What would other people like? Would they find this funny? Would they be appalled if they saw this?'

The importance of organization

Many works of creation are produced without their creators knowing in advance precisely how they would turn out. In *Playwrights on Playwriting*, Arthur Miller, writing about his play *Death of a Salesman*, confessed: 'For myself it has never been possible to generate the energy to write and complete a play if I know in advance everything it signifies and all it will contain. The very impulse to write, I think, springs from an inner chaos crying for order, for meaning, and that meaning must be discovered in the process of writing or the work lies dead as it is finished.' Interestingly enough, Miller describes the driving force of his work as the search for organisation and order and not that all-important quality 'originality'. In the course of an interview with David Ogilvy a similar viewpoint emerged. 'What I abhor is the self-conscious pursuit of originality. It ends up so often in silly pretentious nonsense . . . Originality is the most dangerous word in the lexicon of advertising.'

Jonathan Miller agrees: 'You don't undertake to do a job in

order to be novel. You find yourself overtaken by a problem which seems to you to be irritating until solved, intriguing until dealt with.' In fact Jonathan Miller is particularly iconoclastic about so-called originality. Among scientists, for example, he considers that only very few have the intellectual endowment to shatter paradigms and make scientific revolutions. Paradigm breakers are also very rare in art: 'The number of times that paradigms have been broken can be numbered on the fingers of a fairly badly mutilated hand.'

Jean Muir's work as a designer is a particularly interesting case in point. She does not try to jump too far too soon. She describes herself as an 'evolutionary' (as opposed to revolutionary) designer of fashion. 'I don't play tricks with design and do things to create a furore.' Unlike some of her contemporaries, Muir does not suddenly spring on the public some outrageous features or colours or shades simply in order to look new or different, even though these qualities are the necessary qualities of a successful collection. She manages instead to find innovation within convention. The need to discover novelty must be intrinsic to a creative work, even if it is not pursued self-consciously: 'Change and innovation is a fundamental part of the creative process in design. You're not prepared to accept the status quo. You want to move things on' (Stephen Bayley).

A creative personality?

Clearly, from all the remarks made by creative people in the course of this chapter, there is a lot of common ground between them in the way that they view their activities. And this is despite the fact that they may be very different as individuals. Creative people can, like anyone else, be strong- or weak-minded; decent or immoral; sensitive or brutish in their relationships; educated or untutored; religious or atheists and so on. It is difficult to find in short a creative personality as such. But for Stephen Bayley certain character traits are imperative: 'Creative people need to have a sort of vision and a strong moral commitment to changing things for the better. They have to be unafraid of breaking rules, although it's axiomatic that they have to know the rules in the first place. So they have to be disciplined people.' Jean Muir comments: 'Single-mindedness, stamina both mental and physical, not getting diverted by transient moods or fads or critics, sticking to what you know.' For David Ogilvy a few more traits can be added: 'A sense of humour. I've never known anybody without a sense of humour producing big ideas . . . ungovernable curiosity about a wide range of subjects is another thing . . . It's setting high standards and sticking to them. Not settling for muck. Being straightfor-ward and candid. Having an atmosphere of lunacy. A kind of crazy mad atmosphere. Well-organized people are dull dogs. They're not creative at all . . . ' Mind you, adds Ogilvy, spotting the creative person can be difficult as he knows from his own experience! 'I can remember one of my sisters saying to me: "You're a big faker. You're the most uncreative man who ever lived. You've never had an idea in your life." '

And what about the popular notion that creative people are driven by their angst-ridden desire to discharge unwanted feelings through their art or craft? 'I don't think so,' reflects Michael Frayn. 'I suppose I'm a mildly depressive sort of person, but not acutely so. I don't think I've got a manic side.' On the other hand, Frayn recognizes that writing can have a 'therapeutic' effect: 'When something's going well, I get a sense of elation, a feeling of being released in some way, finding powers that I didn't know I had. I suppose that's why it's so awful when it goes badly.'

Jonathan Miller draws on his medical training in his assessment of a connection between creativity and psycho-logical disorder: 'My own view of the relationship between mental illness of whatever sort and art and science is that they usually proceed in spite of it, not because of it . . . I don't believe in either divine or pathological frenzy as a source of creation. There are artists who happen to have been depressed, frenzied or manic, and who also happen to be geniuses. But their genius does not flow from their disorder. It's something they manage to live with and to produce with. The idea that you have to be in some way disordered to produce or that it's an advisable state of mind is . . . nonsense.'

A gift or a skill?

Throughout this book it is argued that the conventional notion of creativity as a gift from the capricious gods looks, on close inspection, decidedly shaky. Creativity may be seen more as a skill than a gift. Do creative people themselves agree?

'You can teach creativity by example, in the same way that you can teach people to be moderately good writers even if they have no literary skill or aspirations . . . Creativity is something to do with morals. It's being prepared to break rules. It's something to do with being able to sustain failure, but still be able to go on. Always having a different idea, not always better, sometimes worse. Constant movement and change' (Stephen Bayley).

'It's a continuous process of making . . . fashioning' (Jean Muir).

Summary

In this chapter we have discovered many similarities in the ways creative people approach their work. Most of them agree that:

1 · Being well organized is vital.

2 · Discipline and self-criticism are also vital.

3 · It is no good waiting for the bolt from the blue – hard work is needed.

4 · Worrying about being unable to come up with ideas is part of the process.

5 · Outside stimuli can help, but so can internal tensions.

6 · A little knowledge is better than none, but best of all is a great deal of it.

In the next chapter we will explore the net of nerves inside our skulls that makes creativity possible in the first place.

6

INSIDE THE
CREATIVE BRAIN

In a jar in a laboratory in Wichita sits Albert Einstein's brain. The interesting thing about it – apart from the fact that it is still in existence – is that it is remarkably average. In size, in shape, in the degree of corrugations covering its surface it is unremarkable. The average brain weighs about 1400 grams. Some men of genius have had brains much larger. The Russian writer Ivan Turgenev, for instance, is about the weightiest individual on record. His skull contained over 2000 grams' worth of brain. Anatole France, on the other hand, had to perform his works of creation with a mere 1016 grams. Among the brains of famous men which have been preserved, there appears to be no direct connection between size and ability. Whatever creativity is, it apparently does not depend on brute brain capacity.

1400 grams of human brain contain over a hundred thousand million nerve cells, or neurones, each of which can make connections to thousands of others. Modern techniques of electrophysiology can trace the connections between these cells. An astonishing tangle seems to emerge. On the face of it, neurones appear to be attached to others almost at random. Yet we now know that there is great organization present in the brain. As the organ develops, nerve cells send out filaments. These connect with great precision to target nerve cells. It turns out that the target cells are precisely those they will need to communicate with in order to make the adult organism work properly.

At the moment, we do know a certain amount about how we see things, or smell them, about the chemical systems that modify our moods and how our reflexes work.

In these cases, there appears to be little difficulty in at least understanding how an outside event, such as a pin-prick in the arm, or a sound in the ears, can generate a host of responses. The best known case is, of course, the knee-jerk reflex. Here, striking the tendon just below the kneecap sends a nervous signal up to the spinal cord. There it is directed

THE REFLEX ARC

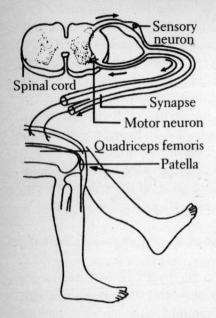

The knee jerk reflexes in which a tap on the knee stimulates stretch receptors in the quadriceps femoris muscle. This impulse is passed to the spinal cord, where a single synapse passes the impulse to the motor nerve to flex the muscle.

Source: B. Dixon (ed.), *Health and the Human Body*. Perseus Press, 1986, p. 57.

back down to the muscles of the thigh. They contract, and the leg twitches. An automatic response, clearly without any intervention from conscious thought. Try it and see if you can stop it.

Other reflexes, particularly those which have been taught, or conditioned, can generate more complex responses. Train a dog to associate the sound of a ringing bell with the appearance of food. There already exists a reflex in dogs – and in people for that matter – that will produce saliva in response to the appearance of food. Now ring the bell but withhold the food. The sound in the dog's ears will stimulate the parts of the brain concerned with hearing. They in turn will stimulate those connected with salivation. The dog will be disappointed, but he will still respond with saliva as if a plate of steak were in front of him.

It is possible to see here the similarities with the automatic knee-jerk. But in the case of thinking, or imagining something new, it is much harder to unravel the brain processes involved. So hard, in fact, that it has not yet been accomplished. There is no doubt that there is nervous activity within the brain during thinking. In his 1984 Reith Lectures on BBC Radio, the American philosopher John Searle argued that: 'Mental phenomena, all mental phenomena whether conscious or unconscious, visual or auditory, pains, tickles, itches, thoughts, indeed all of our mental life, are caused by processes going on in the brain.'

It has become possible to detect characteristic patterns of nervous activity in the brain by attaching electrodes to the scalps of volunteers and recording the changes in the electrical signals generated when they are asked to perform some task. In some of the most interesting of these experiments, Steven Hillyard and his colleagues at the University of California at San Diego asked their volunteers to listen to sentences whose sense depended on the last word in the sentence. The classic example of a nonsense sentence was, 'He spread the warm bread with socks.' The brain generates a characteristic signal about four-tenths of a second after hearing this sentence. It does not do so when the sentence makes sense. Just about all of us know how to tell sense from nonsense. These studies show that there is a physical basis for our ability to discern. Nerve cells in the brain seem to respond selectively to things that make sense, and ignore things that do not.

Other studies give us more detailed information about the locations where thinking takes place, to the extent that there is now no doubt that certain areas of the brain are connected with certain specific thinking tasks. As early as the end of the nineteenth century, Sir Charles

Sherrington and C. S. Roy hypothesized that there must be some mechanism which would provide specific areas of the brain with increased blood supply when they were active. In other words, during thinking or remembering, certain parts of the brain would become engorged with blood.

The development of techniques for forming images of the functioning brain suggested that Roy and Sherrington were substantially correct. These methods opened a new window into the activity of the brain. They were based on the premise that every time a nerve emits an impulse, it must consume a minute amount of energy. If scientists could track in the brain the places where energy was being consumed during thinking, they would be able to see which areas were involved.

In the 1960s, David Ingvar and Niels Lassen, working in Sweden and Denmark, developed a way to make this technique work. They honed it to the point where it could be used to track the blood flow to surface areas of the brain. The technique was taken up by Per Roland and his colleagues in Copenhagen. In a series of experiments, Roland injected into the bloodstreams of volunteers a tiny quantity of a radioactive gas, xenon 133, dissolved in liquid. The head was surrounded with an array of detectors sensitive to radioactive emissions. The xenon 133 was carried in the bloodstream to the brain. The radiation was released as the blood passed through the brain: the more blood, the more radiation could be detected. The flow through particular areas of the brain could therefore be measured. Roland has continued his experiments, and has been able to demonstrate that different parts of the cerebral cortex receive increased blood flow during different types of thinking. If the volunteer tries to recall something from visual memory – a face, or a photograph, for example – then a part of the brain towards the back, called the superior parietal lobe, will become active, as well as other parts towards the front in the frontal lobe.

Leopard Drawings by Jonathan Kenworthy

4b

5

6

7 Jonathan Kenworthy's bronze leopard

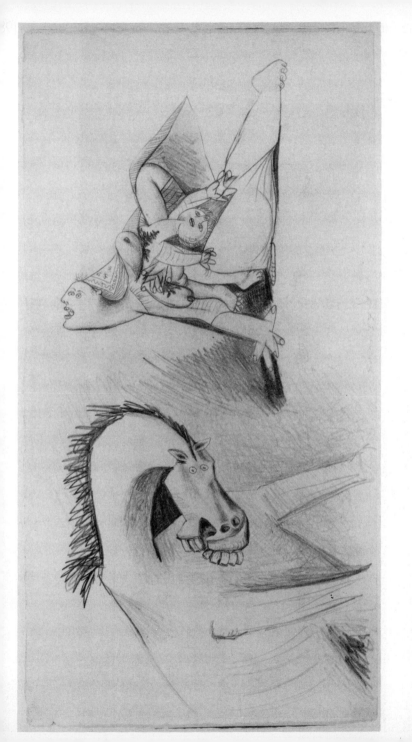

Picasso's *Guernica*   Prado, Madrid © DACS 1988

If asked to recall some *words*, though, then the part called the temporal lobe will demand more blood flow. Similarly, if presented with a mathematical problem, say, start with 50 and then subtract 3 until you cannot subtract it any more, then the superior frontal cortex and the supramarginal cortex needed about one-third more blood. And when subjects were asked to recite a nonsense jingle, but missing out every second word, then the temporal lobe received more blood, and a different pattern of blood flow emerged in the frontal lobe to that seen when verbal memory was engaged. The typical increase in flow when the subjects were using their memories was about 30 per cent.

Remembering something clearly demands a lot of energy. Who said thinking is not hard work?

One of the intriguing things Roland found was that there was no increase in activity during these purely mental tasks in any of the areas of the brain concerned with the senses. These areas are left totally cold. Nor is any activity seen in any of the areas concerned with movement, the motor areas. Thoughts, then, can be generated and exist without outside stimulation, and without the need to respond to the environment.

Roland has his doubts about how far the technique can be pushed, expressed during an interview on BBC Radio in 1984. Can it, for example, tell us anything about subtle aspects of moral thought, or of religion, or about the future or the past?

We expected that these thoughts would be very subtle, that we wouldn't be able to catch them with this method. It turns out that things that can be solved very easily by a little chip on a computer take up large areas of the brain, because the brain doesn't work like a computer. We can see the types of thinking that are going on in the brain, but we cannot really see the contents of people's minds, the contents of thoughts. So we can see in what direction he directs his thoughts, what is the problem he is trying to solve, the general character of the problem. Is he trying to recruit some information from visual memory, and use that in his processing? But we cannot see exactly what is the scenery that he's recruiting to do his thinking.

What Roland's and similar studies seem to show is that certain conscious processes – even those we think of as artistic – reside in certain specific parts of the brain. The disadvantage of this method is that it can look at events only on the surface of the brain. The deep parts are inaccessible. Positron Emission Tomography, or PET scanning, removes that restriction. In principle, PET scanning is similar to the procedure adopted by Roland. Instead of xenon 133, PET scanning takes advantage of compounds which emit positively charged particles, or positrons. These compounds are normally used, or broken down, by the body's metabolic processes. As they break down, positrons are emitted. The positrons meet normal, negatively charged electrons. The two annihilate, and the result is two beams of radiation, or gamma rays, that emerge in opposite directions from the head.

An array of detectors around the body picks up the rays. The information is fed to a computer, which is able to reconstruct an image of the activity deep inside the brain. It is almost as if a slice had been taken through the brain, and the active elements displayed for study. This technique is extremely promising for the future. So far a number of experiments appear to have confirmed the existence of functional localizations. Investigations conducted recently by the psychiatrist Richard Haier of the University of California, Irvine, have shown, for instance, that certain personality traits – including neuroticism, psychoticism and sensation-seeking – can be localized to particular regions of the brain.

Another study explored what was going on in the brains of people working on a difficult abstract reasoning task. Some subjects were more intelligent than others, and hence performed better on the test. These intelligence differences were reflected directly in the action of their neurones. Surprisingly, the more intelligent the individual, the *fewer* brain cells he or she called into operation to perform the task. Perhaps, speculates Dr Haier, differences in intelligence are therefore the result of variations in neuronal efficiency, a case of 'the fewer neurones the better', or, more succinctly, 'more is less'.

Other scanning techniques are also illuminating areas of the brain in different ways. Nuclear Magnetic Resonance, or NMR, imaging allows complex physiological and chemical events within the brain to be monitored as they proceed. Perhaps in the future, NMR imaging, and other, even more exotic techniques, will reveal the site of generation of original ideas.

Thinking on both sides of the brain

In the 1960s, Roger Sperry, Michael Gazzaniga, and Joseph Bogen began a series of experiments that seemed to pin down certain types of thinking to certain parts of the brain. They were studying patients in which the great bundle of connecting fibres between the two hemispheres of the brain – the corpus callosum – had been cut in an effort to reduce the severity of epileptic attacks.

The epilepsy was cured to a large extent, but there were peculiar side effects. The two hemispheres appeared to behave differently. The left appeared to be responsible for language and for logical thought. The right seemed to hold sway over artistic abilities and intuition; and, some would say, creativity. There is now extensive information available about the behaviour of people with split brains.

On the face of it, the hypothesis is attractive. One half of the brain controls our inspirational, creative life. The other is logical, rational, and controlled. They talk to each other through the corpus callosum, and a balanced individual emerges. Not everyone agrees with this hypothesis, however. There are those who do not believe in a single locus of creativity in the right hemisphere. The psychologist Robert Ornstein, for instance, has written: 'Perhaps creativity is not general at all but is domain specific: a different function dependent upon the part of the mind that is active. It would not surprise me to find that the products of creation are very different in talking, moving, and mathematics.' Howard Gardner of Harvard University, also a psychologist, has developed a theory of multiple intelligences, each devoted to a specific task.

Michael Gazzaniga, one of the original investigators who studied the split-brain patients, is also now coming closer to this view. In his recent book *The Social Brain* he does what he calls 'Left-brain Right-brain mania: a debunking'. He then puts forward his own theory that the mind is made up of a number of modules, and that 'most of those modules are capable of actions, moods, and responses'.

By way of example, he cites the case of one patient whose passion was drawing cars. Drawing is said to be controlled by the 'creative' right half of the brain. But movements of the right hand are under the control of the *left* half. If, then, you were to sever the connections between the hemispheres, the nerve impulses from the 'creative' right half would, in theory at least, be unable to pass from the right side through the left and on to the right hand. Thus no artistic drawing would be possible. But with this patient it *was*. After the two halves of his brain were separated, he was still able to draw superb pictures, even though he was then unable to guide his right hand from his right hemisphere. Gazzaniga goes on:

Special talents like those seen (in this case) can reside in the right brain or the left. Clearly, what is important is not so much where things are located, but that specific brain systems handle specific tasks. We begin to see that the brain has a modular nature, a point that comes out of all the data. It is of only secondary interest that the modules should always be in the same place.

Per Roland also had his doubts arising from the accuracy of his studies of localization:

Basically, both sides of the brain are activated no matter what task you put them to. There are, however, differences in the intensity by which the blood flow goes up. For instance if one is trying to explain something, then the left, so-called broker area, would be more activated, the blood flow would go up more here than in the right counterpart, so there are some intensity differences, but the very big differences we don't see. Likewise in the parietal cortex, if people are trying to discriminate tones or musical elements, then the right inferior parietal lobe is activated, whereas the left is not. There are smaller differences in the patterns, but not the very big ones that one would expect from the split-brain studies. So, under normal conditions when the brain functions, both hemispheres work very closely together.

The further use of techniques such as Per Roland's may eventually reveal whether creative thought can be pinned down not only to one hemisphere, but to a particular area within it. So far, though, no one has studied systematically which parts become active when ideas are spontaneously generated. There are, of course, profound difficulties in conducting such an experiment. One of the few certain things about creative thinking is that it is very rarely done to order. To perform creatively under the stress of an experiment is asking a great deal of the subject.

Given the amount of research effort now being devoted to understanding the workings of the mind and brain, it would be surprising if some enterprising group of researchers does not attempt such a study soon.

A set of studies which are unlikely to be repeated – on creative artists at any rate, despite their profound importance – were those undertaken by the Canadian neurosurgeon Wilder Penfield in the 1940s. Penfield was also attempting to treat serious cases of epilepsy by removing the parts of the brain thought to cause the seizures, like the cases that led to the split-brain studies mentioned earlier.

First he had to identify the area responsible. His method was to stimulate the surface of the exposed brain with a weak electric current. He hoped to find a point at which the stimulation would mimic some of the sensations that preceded an attack. He would then destroy that part of the brain. The technique worked, and as a by-product it allowed Penfield to explore the functions of other parts of the brain.

He could, for example, make the patients' muscles contract, or make them see points of light. But more importantly, he found that he could elicit events in the patients' lives that they had forgotten by attaching his electrodes to the parts of the brain called the temporal lobe and the hippocampus. The memories were detailed and clear. What emerged depended on the exact part of the brain that was being excited. More recently, in experiments which echo those performed by Steven Hillyard, Dr Eric Halgren of the University of California at Los Angeles has been able to look at the actions of individual nerve cells in responding to sense or nonsense. Also working with patients undergoing surgery for epilepsy, he and his colleagues have been able to measure the electrical response of single neurones to sentences which make either sense or nonsense. Their results too seem to indicate that single cells can tell the difference between something which makes sense about the world, and something which does not. It appears, then, that complex sets of thoughts can be generated by quite small changes in the local electrical activity of the nervous system.

But where might thoughts come from when there is no outside stimulation? How can the mass of nerve cells generate spontaneous activity? Worse than that, how can this activity be about the world? Or make any sort of sense?

The answer is that we don't know where ideas come from. People have, of course, had ideas. In his book *Neuronal Man*, the French neurophysiologist Jean-Pierre Changeux has described the chemical and electrical process whereby nerve cells can oscillate between two states, even without any outside stimulation. He went on: 'This spontaneous activity could, of course, be at the root of the "internal" genesis of mental objects and their linking together without interaction with the outside world.'

Perhaps Changeux is right. Perhaps there is constant, almost random activity going on in nerve cells. Occasionally, it will add up to something that exceeds the threshold of consciousness, and we will become aware of it. So is that all there is to creative thought? Letting the machine turn over until something emerges?

This was roughly the position of the behaviourist school of psychology. Behaviourism was largely the creation of John B. Watson between the two world wars. It held that it makes no sense to ask about what goes on inside the head. Consider only the influences acting on, and the responses generated by, the person. This 'black box' approach proved sterile in explaining the ways people behave. But perhaps there is a grain of validity in it in this case.

The phrenologists attempted to evaluate the qualities of a person by measuring the contours of the outside of the skull.

They assigned certain attributes to certain portions of the brain. Only now have we come to recognize and investigate the localized functions of the brain. In the same way, perhaps at least the random generation of new ideas proposed by the behaviourists might still have some relevance.

The act of creation

What appears to characterize an act of creation is that it allows us to see the world in a new way. It also, as we have seen, draws on the experiences and memories of the creator. How, then, might these everyday occurrences – and in some cases not so everyday – be transformed into something fresh and original?

In Chapter 5 we saw that many creative people consider organization to be one of their most valuable attributes. It enables them to gain access to information easily. And information is the currency of ideas. Perhaps creative people might have more efficient memories than the rest of us? There are two lines of evidence that might prove illuminating.

In the 1960s, researchers into artificial intelligence at MIT were trying to make machines that could solve problems in mathematics. One of them, James Schlagel, designed a program that could solve problems in undergraduate calculus. The students found these sorts of problems hard to deal with, but the program could do at least as well as the humans in finding solutions. Had the scientists made an intelligent – even a creative – machine?

It turned out that the key to the program's success was information. All it needed was about 100 facts about the problem area it was working in, and a fairly simple logical processor. It was so simple that it caused some to wonder what was wrong with the educational system if so many students could not master such a seemingly trivial skill.

The important thing here, though, is that access to information allows problems to be solved.

There is a second example from AI. When researchers started to make expert systems – that is systems that mimic the behaviour of a human expert in some field – they faced a problem. How could they find out how the human experts were actually solving problems? A new field was developed. Called knowledge engineering, its purpose was to extract from human problem-solvers the essence of their skill. There now exist expert systems in many fields, including medicine, prospecting, end-game playing in chess, and so on. In some cases the machine can outperform the man.

How? The key, again, is access to information. The researchers found that the main difference between the human expert and an ordinary performer was simply that the expert knew more. As Marvin Minsky, the cognitive scientist of MIT, puts it: 'An expert doesn't have to think, he knows.'

We would find it unsatisfactory to believe that the keys to creation were merely there to unlock a store of existing information. But there is no doubt that the 'blank slate' view of creativity is even more unsatisfactory. According to this, it is better not to know about the field in which you propose to create. Should you do so you will blunt the edge of your originality by forcing your own thought patterns into lines similar to those used by others in the field. Only from the blank state can something new and fresh emerge.

Again, as we have seen in Chapter 5, creative people do not find this idea appealing. They all acknowledge that they benefit from knowing the history not only of their own area of enterprise, but of others. Again, the key is information. But obviously, the information is no good unless it can be used. It must be available to be teased into different shapes, to have unthought-of connections imposed on it. Here is where the particular organization of the brain might again have unique value.

The human brain appears to work on information in a parallel fashion. That is, it can hold and process many items of information at the same time. To see something, for instance, requires the simultaneous processing of thousands upon thousands of pieces of information about the world outside. When we consider the way our memories work, we come across a similar phenomenon. We do not have to search in a logical, linear fashion for a particular piece of memory. Often, just one thought can spark a train of others, all somehow connected to the first, but at different degrees of remoteness from it. Could it be here that one of the roots of creation lies – the ability of our brains to make connections effortlessly between different parts of our experience? And could it be that the creative brain is one which is particularly adept at making these connections?

The second line of evidence comes from work done by Dr Christopher Brand of Edinburgh University. He was interested in how the brains of people with different measured levels of intelligence would respond to simple events: how quickly they could discriminate between two sounds at different pitches, or between two lines of different lengths. Brand found that people who score highly on IQ tests are also able to make their judgements more quickly than those whose measured IQs are low. Brand's view is that quickness of response points to a better brain mechanism for correlating and processing information. The significance of these results is a matter of controversy.

It may be, though, that the creative brain has elements of all these attributes. It is better constructed for processing information; the rate at which it can do it is faster than that within the non-creative brain; and its internal organization facilitates connections between disparate elements in its memory.

Summary

1 · There is plenty of evidence for a tangible connection between electrical activity in the brain and thought. There is no need to invoke a 'ghost in the machine' to impel ideas into us.

2 · There is also good evidence that certain parts of the brain do certain tasks. Language and memory in particular would seem to be localized.

3 · There is no evidence for any creative centre in the brain. In fact, even the notion that we do all our creative thinking in the right hemisphere is now coming under attack.

4 · It is possible that ideas are only the random firings of nerve cells that reach sufficient strength to leave the realm of the unconscious. Once in the conscious mind, the idea must be tested against the real world before its worth can be evaluated.

5 · Where do ideas come from in the brain? No one knows, but in a few years with the aid of PET scanning and other imaging techniques we should be much closer to finding out.

7

STRATEGIES FOR CREATIVITY

Highly creative people, in whatever field they express their talent, are apparently very rare. Only a tiny fraction of the population seems, at first glance, to be endowed with the precious quality. And yet, as we saw in the last chapter, neurologically speaking, creative individuals are nothing special. The brain of a Tolstoy or a Michelangelo would be no different in size, shape or structure from the grey matter of anyone plucked at random off the street.

Another fact that emerges from the study of how the enormous collection of nerve cells of the brain behaves, is that we all have a good deal of inbuilt cerebral redundancy. We have vastly more than enough neurones for coping with the many tasks handled by the brain. Thus we can, to some extent, afford to lose the use of quite large populations of cells without becoming devoid of brain function, because substitute armies of dedicated (in the sense of specialized) neurones are immediately conscripted to step into the breach.

Pondering, then, on these two features of the brain – its uniformity and its superabundance of available, but often unused, cells – it is tempting to speculate on how many spectacular intellectual abilities, of which creativity is a prime example, might be available to the majority of us. Could we, in short, deliberately set out to exploit the under-used potential of the human brain? It is an ambitious idea, and it is not at all as clear-cut as some people might have us believe. We have all seen those newspaper and magazine advertisements offering us the 'Keys to Unlocking the Power of the Mind' or the 'Hidden Mysteries of the Brain'. Many a client has sent away for the seductive package only to be disappointed with its contents. Expecting to find some kind of secret 'formula' for instantly switching the brain into a higher gear, the eager self-improver finds instead some instructions on how to train the brain through hard, regular practice.

There is nothing instantaneous about acquiring an

'Instant Memory': nothing rapid about displaying a 'Quick Mind'. It is well established by psychologists that certain areas of human performance can be enhanced by applying well-tried principles. To improve memory, for example, one can learn to categorize and subsequently recall information using various mnemonics. If you want to remember a list of key words in economics such as Market, Inflation, Exchange Rates and so on, you mentally construct a story or a picture deliberately involving these terms. Thus you might imagine a picture of a market square, over which floats a swollen balloon (Inflation), while down below two people are giving each other boxes marked 'Rates' and so on. The more amusing or bizarre the scenarios one builds around the material to be remembered, the better your chances of recalling it. Some mnemonists are able to construct fantastically complex 'hierarchies' of ideas in this way, starting with basic concepts and working up to high-level variations.

By application, then, it is possible to channel our brains into serving us better so far as memory is concerned. The same may be true of creativity, providing we adopt the right strategies.

Strategy is not ritual

Best-selling authors are constantly receiving letters from aspiring writers, asking them how they do it. Actually what they often ask is not this at all but in what circumstances they prefer to write: what make of typewriter or word processor they use; what kind of paper; whether they work in the mornings or the afternoons, or both; whether they need this or that type of chair, and so on. This is to confuse the preparatory rituals of creation with the act of creativity itself.

Undoubtedly many creative people do have these characteristic, often quaint, ways of getting down to work. Like the long-jumper or boxer with his repetitive, minutely detailed preliminary routines, a writer might go through necessary little rituals before he or she feels comfortable. Georges Simenon, the prolific author of the Inspector Maigret stories, would assiduously arrange a stack of well-sharpened pencils on his desk before writing. Graham Greene the novelist only feels at ease with one type of writing paper and a particular kind of felt-tipped pen.

In other creative fields, too, ritual plays an important role. People like to put on their favourite piece of Sinatra or Bizet, to sit in a certain battered armchair, to toy with a bunch of keys or a paperweight, all in order to focus the mind on a particular problem or project. Like the mystical mantra of the transcendental meditation, such rituals seem to act as aids to triggering the desired psychological state of awareness and concentration.

However, there is little insight into the creative process itself to be gleaned from such practices. For one thing, many composers, scientists and writers do not behave in this way at all. They can work in any surroundings – given a reasonable degree of peace and quiet (though not always is even this necessary), use any materials that come to hand, and never resort to talisman-style props for the psyche. They are flexible and relaxed where others are consistent and tense. They find it easy to start painting or playing or whatever, where others pace around anxiously before feeling able to commit themselves.

Although ritual obviously plays an important part in the lives of some creative people then, it is not universal. Nor is it transferable. One person's creative mantra will usually not be effective for someone else. So, even if those earnest young writers were to copy scrupulously the bizarre preparatory behaviour of the highly paid best-sellers, it would probably do them no good. Even if it did, it would not create an instantaneous channel into new or original ideas. Ritual can be a way of getting started. It might help you to produce vast amounts of output. But none of it may necessarily be of high quality. For a truly creative strategy we have to look in a somewhat different direction.

Flexible minds

Consider this problem. A man is lying in the middle of a field. Beside him is a package. What has happened? To play this parlour game you need to be able to ask questions of someone who knows the solution to the problem. He or she can answer only 'Yes' or 'No'. When four adults were given this puzzle they spent seven or eight minutes firing questions of all descriptions, eventually getting round to the notion that the man in the field is dead; that the package would have saved his life; that it was to be worn in some way; that it contained in fact an unopened parachute. To reach this conclusion – the correct answer – the adult players had posed an elaborate roundabout series of questions, many of which, when answered, only seemed to complicate the problem still further.

When two young people – one ten years old, the other sixteen – were given the same problem, they solved it in twenty seconds flat. In rapid-fire succession out tumbled questions such as: Is he dead? Did he drop from the sky? They used none of the convoluted, Sherlock Holmes-style reasoning beloved of adults, but went straight into a broad sweep attempt to impose on the given data a feasible story. Typically, this is the style of thinking that advancing years seem to inhibit or suppress. Young minds like young limbs seem often to be more flexible than those of their seniors.

On the face of it, it would seem that flexibility of mind, that ability to leap sideways, upwards and downwards around a problem before reaching a solution, might be an integral part of the creative process. How far is this assumption justified? We need to consider this carefully, because if flexibility is intrinsic to creativity, then here is a positive strategy we might deploy. It is possible to improve one's performance on tasks such as the Parachute Problem by practice. Could this also be a route to enhancing our level of creativity?

The diverger debate revisited

As we saw in Chapter 3, it is tempting to think of the original, creative mind as belonging to a person who thinks in a divergent fashion. The converger, on the face of it, seems to be limited, stereotyped or rigid in the way he or she thinks about the world and hence unlikely to come up with the sort of flexible responses thought to generate original and therefore creative ideas. Unfortunately this tidy dichotomy, we now know, is not altogether acceptable when you apply it to creative people.

In extensive studies of famous scientists, architects and writers, psychologists have found that sometimes it is the diverger who reaches high levels of creativity, sometimes the converger. What appears to matter is the nature of the work they are doing: among the scientists, those working in the physical sciences show more convergent traits than biologists or social scientists. On the other hand, even among the convergers, there is undoubtedly a strong element of open-mindedness and uninhibited thinking. Otherwise they would probably not have made their creative mark on the world. Take for example the remarkably productive scientific output of two outstanding researchers. One is Nobel laureate Francis Crick, who, together with James Watson, published in 1953 a paper in the journal *Nature* which changed science as dramatically as anything from the pen of Newton or Darwin. It was a brief description of the molecule DNA – the building block of all living creatures. The genetic code had at last been cracked. The other researcher headed the celebrated Molecular Biology Laboratory in Cambridge. He is Dr Sydney Brenner, known internationally for his exceptional contribution to the development of genetic manipulation techniques in medical research. Brenner can be regarded, like Crick, as a founding father of the genetic revolution that has swept so rapidly round the world in the past decade or two. As it happens, these two luminaries used to share an office in Cambridge and they used to talk to each other a great deal about anything and everything. It was not all serious, scientific conversation. Far from it. Crick and Brenner would often tell each other jokes; try out sometimes shaky ideas; speculate, fantasize, dream. There were no rules governing what they said; no formal logic to shape their thoughts. Like any normal good friends they simply said whatever came into their heads, however crazy it seemed. From the strictly scientific point of view this anarchic kaleidoscope of notions and concepts might seem fairly useless. In fact, Brenner recalls, it was a fruitful source of inspiration for new ideas, some of which were to endure as important contributions to their fields of research.

Although trained scientists, conditioned not to move ahead too quickly without checking on the solidity of their advances nor jump to attractive but unjustified conclusions, both Crick and Brenner found their free-and-easy, even facile, exchanges highly productive. They were liberated from the normal constraints imposed by their discipline (even that very word 'discipline' is authoritarian) and able to contemplate what scientists sometimes call the 'blue skies'. Of course, once a concept that seemed initially appealing was taken seriously on board, it had to be rigorously subjected to every hard-headed scrutiny imaginable. Some survived the examination. Many did not. But as a method of generating new ideas, Brenner and Crick had found a useful technique that gave them considerable mental flexibility. What is more, their experience demonstrates the apparent Converger/Diverger Paradox. The converging, logical, tramline-minded scientist can co-exist with the flexible, innovative, dreamer artist in one individual. Both styles can live alongside each other, feed on each other, indeed. What is needed is a catalyst to get them to interact.

Creative styles: a study in contrasts

Creating is by definition something positive. It requires action, taking initiatives, having a shot at a target or project. But it can be tackled in quite different ways. At the Occupational Research Centre at the Hatfield Polytechnic, not far from London, Michael Kirton has identified two distinct types of creative individuals, the 'Adaptors' and the 'Innovators'. The Adaptor is the person who reaches a creative end by accepting initially the generally recognized theories, policies or viewpoints around him. He then works outwards towards an innovative and valuable alternative.

Innovators, on the other hand, immediately strike out for fresh territory by detaching the problem they are tackling from its 'cocoon of accepted thought' and looking for a solution unfettered by convention. Both types are equally creative. Although the Innovator might seem, on the face of it, to be the true 'creator' by conforming to the Romantic image of the lone thinker battling against prejudice or fashion, this is far from the truth, argues Dr Kirton.

Take, for example, the fact that in medieval times it seemed impossible to reconcile the observed movement of planets with the then prevailing theories about the structure of the universe. Two different solutions were produced – one Adaptive, one Innovative. The Adaptive approach was to keep the existing theory and invent complicated, supplementary planetary motions to fit in with it. The Innovative thinkers, in contrast, jettisoned convention and moved the earth away from the centre of the cosmos.

As it happens the Innovators were right, but the Adaptors were still quite brilliantly creative in their thinking. What is more there are plenty of examples that show the benefits of high-grade adaptive thinking in creatively resolving problems or affecting change. Dr Kirton arrived at these conclusions through studying the work of managers in radically changing their companies. He looked at such changes as the introduction of new products or reorganization of accounting procedures that had profound effects on the commercial health and business perspectives of the companies involved.

Here too he found that there was no difference in the quality of the innovations proposed by his two types of creative individuals. Both came up with valuable changes that enhanced the performance of their companies. The differences lay in what sorts of problems they addressed in the first place. Adaptors, for example, are at their best in refining existing systems, improving them and extending the thinking that underlies them. They can be relied on to work thoroughly and systematically through various ways of doing things better, to keep risks to a minimum and generally not to make waves within the firm.

The Innovator, of course, does cause ripples throughout the organization. He tends to recommend changes that are difficult to predict, often hard to implement, and to be more abrasive than the Adaptor in presenting his solutions. He thrives on turbulence. He can be erratic and impulsive where the Adaptor is calm and smooth. He can even be potentially dangerous to an organization because he is an advocate of radicalism, whereas the Adaptor's one-step-at-a-time approach is never likely to bring trouble.

In fact both types of creative managers are of use within the same organization: indeed together they produce a healthily balanced agent for change. As with the convergers and divergers, being primarily an Adaptor does not rule out a streak of the Innovator in any of us. Most people anyway are not at one extreme or the other but somewhere in between. We often switch between two modes of behaving, being unpredictable on occasions and systematic on others. We can be careful planners in one context and devil-may-care in another.

Indeed we have to be. A brilliant Innovator would soon find himself out of a job if his proposals for organizational change embittered every single member of the board. The skilful Adaptor, too, would be seeking alternative employment if he allowed his natural caution to close his eyes to a glaring opportunity to act quickly to better his company's lot.

Creativity is a matter of organizing one's basic skills, not regretting that one was not born with a 'quick' or a 'logical' mind. The whizz-kid business executive may, in reality, be no more clever or gifted than the office boy. He succeeds because he has an opportunity to display his qualities, and, if he does, is amply rewarded for them. He is, in short, highly motivated. And without motivation there is little creativity.

Motivation: inner and outer drives

How can creativity be motivated? For the business executive – be he Adaptor, Innovator or whatever – there can be many obvious rewards: promotion, a fat salary increase, a bigger company car and a chance to lunch with the chairman of the board every Thursday. At a humbler level the incentives may be less glamorous but no less attractive; the sales assistant may get a bigger laundry allowance for his or her uniform, or even a free space in the store's car park. Such motivation is essentially extrinsic. It can be useful but it does not always work. In fact it may even be counterproductive.

The poet Sylvia Plath became much concerned over her inability to put words on paper – the classic writer's block.

Eventually she pinned down the trouble to her excessive desire to gain external recognition of her work from editors, publishers, critics and the world at large. 'I want,' she said, 'acceptance there, and to feel my work good and well taken. Which ironically freezes me at my work, corrupts my nunnish labour of work-for-itself-as-its-own-reward.'

In other words, Sylvia Plath came to realize that her most creative work would only emerge if she were intrinsically motivated – to want to write for the sake of it, not to satisfy other people but to please herself. At Brandeis University, Teresa Amabile found something similar as a result of a motivational experiment. She had the assistance of 72 young adults, chosen because they identified themselves as actively involved in creative writing. In the laboratory they were given a poem to write. Then they were assigned to three groups and given a second poem to write. Before doing so however they were asked to fill out a questionnaire. Group One's questions focused on intrinsic reasons for writing – self-satisfaction, the desire to make something beautiful and so on. Group Two's questions turned on extrinsic motivation – winning approval or admiration and the like. Group Three – the control group – was not given a questionnaire at all on their reasons for writing.

When the second poems were completed they were evaluated for their levels of creativity. 'There were,' writes Teresa Amabile, 'significant differences in the creativity of the poems written after the experimental manipulations. Poems written under an extrinsic orientation were significantly less creative than those written in the other two conditions.' These findings are echoed by many well-known creative people. Even though they may have deadlines to meet and need to benefit financially from their work in order to live, they constantly point to the inner motivation of self-satisfaction as their driving force. The awards and the plaudits are secondary. When asked whether she is motivated by being given a lucrative commission, one eminent artist replied: 'A commission is neither here nor there . . . one must love one's work.'

What is true of the creative domains of the arts and the sciences may also be true in the hard-nosed world of business and commercial productivity. In a booklet published by the American Management Association, *Idea Management: How to Motivate Creativity and Innovation*, Charles Clark writes: 'Incentives are effective motivators, but pride, self-respect, and doing something worth while are even more compelling.' Clark goes on to support his case by looking at the phenomenal success of Japanese quality circles – groups of around 8–12 workers who meet in company time to discuss and deal with safety, quality control and production matters in their work area.

Everyone knows of the astonishing progress made by Japanese industry since World War Two, especially in the manufacture of high-quality and precision products. It had to be so if Japan were to thrive. A population of 115 million people – more than twice that of Britain – lives tightly packed in a country only one and a half times as large. They have precious few natural resources and little arable land. The Japanese have to rely on importing resources cheaply and exporting them at a greatly enhanced value in the form of manufactured goods. Today people in all countries of the world instantly recognize that the 'Made in Japan' label is synonymous with excellence and reliability.

In 1979 a team of American industrial managers went under the aegis of the Technology Transfer Institute to find out how the Japanese managed to achieve and sustain their superb quality control. They came back with a variety of reasons. Clearly the quality circle idea is very well suited to Japanese society with its common language and culture and high educational standards. Trade unions are organized so that there is usually only one union per firm. Jobs are relatively secure, with no lay-offs to cloud the horizon. All these factors are undoubtedly relevant to the success of Japan. But the visiting team identified one other that stands out above the rest. Workers are genuinely proud of their work because managers greatly value their participation in the running of the firm.

Workers are encouraged to help in management. 'That workers are taught to think creatively,' writes Charles Clark, 'builds self esteem. To ensure quality the QC (quality circle) is often given a major responsibility in training new workers. In many corporations, the quality circle has a target for submitting a specified number of recommendations each year. Management is then required to implement a specified percentage of those recommendations.'

In other words the commitment of the manager to excellence cascades down throughout the whole company because everyone feels involved in a common purpose, not just on paper but in the reality of the workplace. Workers take pride and care in their work because they can see quite directly their personal contribution to the running of the firm taking effect. They are not cogs in an impersonal machine. Like the craftsman or the painter they see the fruits of their own handiwork. Therein lies their motivation to introduce new ideas for improving the quality of their work. They are profoundly motivated to create.

Safety in numbers: groups or solo?

The effectiveness of Japanese quality circles also suggests another creative strategy: that of pooling intellectual resources by working in groups. Many people value group thinking, or 'brainstorming', very highly indeed. Charles Clark is one. He writes: 'Persons who brainstorm regularly are repeatedly amazed at how the technique stimulates an explosion of ideas, along with strong surges of positive feeling. It's something like the process that takes place inside a nuclear pile.'

Others, though, are less than enthusiastic. The veteran adman David Ogilvy – from his perspective in an industry where group problem-solving strategies are often used – dismisses the whole enterprise. 'Brainstorming? I'll tell you what brainstorming is. It's people who've never had an idea in their life, thinking that if ten of them get together in a room one of them might have an idea. It's an excuse to waste time because there's nothing coming out of them. They're not fertile. They lay eggs which don't hatch. Brainstorming is idiotic.'

Originally the concept of brainstorming grew out of economic and industrial preoccupations. Born on Madison Avenue, the technique began to become popular in the 1950s when Alex Osborn saw it as a route by which the USA might enhance the creativity of its engineers and scientists in the face of the technological Cold War threat from the USSR.

At its simplest, brainstorming means getting a number of people around a table to voice whatever ideas come to them on a particular topic. So, for example, if a group were discussing ways of getting elderly people to take more exercise the suggestions might range from obvious strategies such as 'Take them out for a walk', 'Get schoolchildren volunteers to escort them round the park', 'Ask local athletic or swimming clubs to organize activities' to more unusual solutions such as: 'Install exercise machines in their apartment blocks', 'Bus them or even fly them to a football stadium for mass games' and so on.

In the often wild atmosphere of group sessions (participants are, after all, storming their brains) all kinds of exotic and far-fetched notions are thrown up. There may, in theory at least, be one that itself fits the bill. Or perhaps two or more may be thrown up at the same time, and in combination, they offer a useful, creative solution.

In fact Osborn's view of brainstorming as put forward in his much-discussed book *Applied Imagination*, published in 1953, went a little beyond this. Osborn contended that the creative group would work best if it encouraged totally spontaneous ideas that were immediately offered to the assembly, without any critical or evaluative judgement being applied to them. In other words, no matter how wild the idea it should be expressed.

Osborn proposed five basic brainstorming rules:

1. No one should adversely criticize any one else's idea.
2. The more unusual or even crazy the idea, the better.
3. Aim for quantity of output. The more suggestions put forward, the greater the chances of finding a winner.
4. Ideas can be toyed with. They can be combined and recombined with others or simply adapted to improve them.
5. The group must be interactive. As individuals indulge their imagination and even fantasy, the rest should help them along by offering cues, associations and pointers that will generate still more ideas.

The concept of brainstorming was a timely one. Osborn's ideas spread rapidly. It is estimated that in 15 years over 75 large American corporations had instituted brainstorming training among their personnel. However during that period doubts began to emerge as to whether this new technique really did stimulate creative thinking. Donald Taylor and his colleagues at Yale University carried out an experiment in 1958 with the title 'Does group participation when using brainstorming facilitate or inhibit creative thinking?' Taylor concluded that it did not. Individuals, he reckoned, could solve problems better on their own than in groups.

In 1963, Marvin Dunnette at the University of Minnesota poured even more cold water on the brainstorming movement by updating Taylor's experiment and reaching much the same conclusion.

The Dunnette experiment is worth a closer look. Forty-eight research scientists and 48 advertising personnel employed at the 3M Company were given problems to solve in either a brainstorming or a solo context. The problems were four in number.

In the 'Thumbs' problem participants were asked to imagine what would happen if everyone had an extra thumb on each hand, located on the opposite side to the present thumb. What would be the practical benefits or difficulties in having this extra thumb?

Problem number two concerned 'Education'. Because of the increasing birthrate in the US during the 1940s it is predicted that to preserve current student–teacher ratios in schools, no less than 50 per cent of all college graduates would have to go into teaching. Are there any other steps that could be taken to maintain effective instruction in schools?

Next came the 'People' problem. Suppose that discoveries in medicine and nutrition had the effect of increasing the height of the average 20-year-old American to 6 feet 8 inches, and doubling his weight. What would be the consequences of this state of affairs? What adjustments would have to be made?

Then, finally, comes the 'Tourists' problem. Dunnette's subjects were asked to think up ways of inducing more European tourists to come to the US.

Having divided up his subjects into solo or brainstorming units, and incidentally having arranged things so that individuals could take part in both types, Dunnette then analysed their ideas for both quantity and quality. Sure enough he found that, like Taylor, he tended to disagree with Alex Osborn, who had stated categorically that 'the average person can think up twice as many ideas when working with a group than when working alone'.

In fact there were times when group interaction – at least for the advertising people for whom, ironically, brainstorming was first devised – was positively detrimental. The admen were relatively inhibited in groups. On their own they came up with more ideas, and without sacrificing quality. On the 'Tourists' and 'Education' problems, indeed, their ideas were distinctly better when they worked alone.

This is not the only experiment to suggest that brainstorming is an overvalued creative strategy. Peter Dillon and his colleagues at the University of California, Berkeley, studied the effects of videotaped training sessions on brainstorming groups working on ways to improve US foreign policy. One would have expected such training to facilitate group performance but it did not. Moreover, Dillon found that in general individuals were superior to groups in their creative output.

However, Dillon also noticed something that Dunnette had commented on nearly a decade earlier. The largest number of ideas seemed to spring from individuals whose solo brainstorming followed their participation in a group. It was as if preliminary group work had in a sense primed the pump, allowing the individual to gush forth with ideas in profusion. Whereas a group may fall into a conceptual rut, pursuing the same trains of thought, often to sterile ends, an individual can use some initial group work to limber up intellectually, perhaps to release some of his or her mental inhibitions. Dunnette sums up this finding thus. 'The "best bet" for creative thinking in attacking problems seems, therefore, to be the pooled individual efforts of many people with perhaps an initial group session to serve simply as a warm-up to their efforts.'

Effective brainstorming

In the face of these experiments it would seem that brainstorming groups, which are of course still actively encouraged in many firms, have disappointingly little to offer. At best brainstorming seems to be little more than a preliminary bout of mental calisthenics to limber up the brain for its real business of solo endeavour. According to Professor Thomas Bouchard, however, in the wake of his own experiments at the University of Minnesota, we should be wary of discounting group problem-solving altogether.

True the Dunnette results prick the bubble floated by Osborn thirty years ago but, adds Bouchard, 'they do not disprove the effectiveness of brainstorming as a group problem-solving method. They simply show that individual creativeness is better than group brainstorming *under the conditions imposed by these studies*. There are still some conditions under which group procedures are necessary: when the information for solving a problem is scattered among different people.'

In a series of experiments Bouchard showed that a group's effectiveness depends very much on the way it is allowed to operate. The traditional brainstorming method is fairly anarchic. Everyone and anyone is allowed to chip in with an idea as the humour takes them. Bouchard however tested the performance of groups where each member had to participate sequentially: having spoken he then had to yield to the next speaker or say 'Pass' if he had nothing to contribute that time round.

Comparing the performance of groups conducted in this way with that of individuals, he came up with 'spectacular' results. On average the structured groups generated 87.5 per cent more ideas than unsequenced groups, and exactly the same number of ideas as the average individual performer.

The reasons for this, reckons Bouchard, are threefold:

Sequencing procedures make it difficult for any one individual to dominate the discussion.

They force the discussion to stay on a particular problem, in such a way that all members of the group channel their thoughts along relevant lines.

All members are encouraged, even forced, to become involved. There is no one outstanding member who becomes the 'expert' and inhibits others from contributing.

This last point is critical. When members of a group are conscious of intellectual status differences among them, because one person knows – or appears to know – more than the rest, they are grossly inhibited from expressing themselves. Ironically, then, an unstructured group has an inbuilt 'evaluative' aspect to it which is precisely what conventional brainstorming was supposed to eliminate.

Every committee chairperson knows how difficult it is to prevent these hierarchies from appearing: there is always someone who seems to 'take over' the group, with others falling silent. In the relaxed atmosphere of the bar after a committee meeting the inhibited ones, it turns out, have quite a lot to contribute, but never during the meeting itself.

Thomas Bouchard, then, advocates sequencing as a 'procedural fix' or 'operational strategy' to by-pass the difficulty. Simple but, he contends, effective.

There are other ways in which brainstorming may be made more effective and therefore creative. Before one can hope to produce solutions to any problem it is essential first to define precisely what that problem is. Before finding a solution one has first to find the problem. It is no use letting loose any number of keen minds on a target that is too broad or diffuse to be amenable to a solution anyway.

What one can do is initiate a brainstorming session to define the problem or problems. This is what the US Allied Chemical Corporation did in its attempt to find a way of reducing its huge energy bill. From the company's key 24 industrial processes, analysts selected 5 for special investigation. Teams of engineers then went through a brainstorming session for each process, ultimately combining all their ideas in a 40-page briefing document. This became the agenda for the brainstorm proper, so that participants came to the sessions fully acquainted with the specific character of each of the process areas. To this data base they each lent their individual technical, industrial and commercial expertise, finally coming up with a solution. But it was one in which planning and preparation played an important role.

Another way to improve the quality of a brainstorming session involves the use of certain internal techniques or tricks to open up members' minds. A number of these have been put forward. There is for example the 'lateral thinking' strategy of Edward de Bono, which encourages individuals to look at a problem from a different angle in order to break out of the strait-jacket of convention. 'Lateral thinking,' de Bono writes, 'seeks to get away from the patterns that are leading one in a definite direction and to move sideways by re-forming the patterns.'

In much the same mould is the notion of *synectics* advocated by William Gordon of Synectics Inc. in Cambridge, Mass. The word means joining together two different and apparently unrelated ideas or elements. It involves, too, linking strangeness with familiarity. Confronted with a problem, argues Dr Gordon, we set about trying to make it familiar to us by analysis – drawing on experience to make the transformation. This is understandable, but it may on its own yield only superficial and unimaginative solutions. What is needed is a second step – to make the familiar strange again, by coming up with an original solution.

In order to bring about this change, a number of ploys can be tried. If, for example, one were intent on developing a novel way of packaging a familiar product or of opening a box or a can, the brainstorming team might enact a little play. One member actually plays the part of the product or the container. The others question him in whatever way they choose from their novel perspective. They identify with the task in an engaging fashion.

Thomas Bouchard has tested this 'personal analogy' method of generating ideas with groups working on nine different tasks such as, 'Think up as many names as you can for a new spray deodorant.' One person plays the part of the deodorant. The others contribute ideas, in sequence again, by writing them down on a sheet of paper. The results of such activity, claims Dr Bouchard, are striking: 'The groups that used the personal analogy procedure outperformed the brainstorming groups on all nine tasks.'

Why this should be the case is not at all clear. It could be that the very fact that the 'thinkers' became 'doers' for the purpose of the experiment, being physically active as they played their parts, heightened their creativity. It could be that any new procedure introduced into a brainstorming session acts as a stimulus through sheer novelty value.

Again, though, whether or not a group with a synectic or lateral thinking flavour can outperform an individual is still an open question. What one can say is that group thinking can be improved by sequencing and personal analogy charades. 'They are,' adds Dr Bouchard, 'simple, understandable, fun, require very little training and no special equipment.'

One other useful ingredient which emerges from the work of a number of psychologists is the deliberate use of judgement and criticisms during the group's sessions. Now in Osborn's original scheme of things you will recall that judgements were proscribed. The free flow of one person's ideas, he argued, is impeded by the critical voices of others saying 'It won't work' or even 'It's plumb crazy'. In his excellent study of creativity, Dr Robert Weisberg cites quite a few experiments in which brainstorming group members were set tasks in two modes: one was according to Osborn's non-evaluative procedure; the other contained an instruction to subject ideas to critical analysis and evaluation as they cropped up. In general those groups that subject ideas to searching, critical criteria tend to produce fewer ideas than the more freewheeling groups. However, and this is the important point, in terms of *quality* of ideas emerging, the critical groups are superior in performance. The evidence seems to indicate – though no doubt the idealistic brainstormer of the old school would dispute this – that withholding judgement does nothing to enhance creativity. In fact quite the opposite. The more one can determine what criteria a solution should meet in advance of generating ideas about it, the more one uses those criteria to shape ideas in the first place, the better will that solution be. Robert Weisberg concludes: 'If one wishes to solve a problem effectively, one should try to determine as precisely as possible what criteria the solution must meet before starting work on the problem, try to keep these criteria in mind as one works.' He also adds . . . 'and work alone'.

Analogy and visualization

If someone were to come up to you in the street and ask for some complicated directions to a place on the other side of town you can either rely on a purely verbal description or you can pull out a scrap of paper and draw a rudimentary map. Even something quite crudely drawn will be useful. It does not have to be to scale nor even to shape. If it gets across the general relationship of one landmark to another it will have served a valuable purpose.

The most famous example of such a visualization is the map of the London Underground system. It no more represents the actual network than a line drawing of the heart does justice to the complexity of the circulatory system. But it has steered countless millions of strangers from one end of a very big city to the other in perfect order for many years.

Pictures can help to fix ideas. In fact any symbolic representation can help to give shape to an idea in someone's head. You could listen for a long time to a description of the structure of the DNA molecule that builds up all living organisms. But the pictorial analogy 'like a screw' tells you more or less the whole story instantly.

Research on the creative process in science suggests that many eminent scientists have used analogical visualizations as a source of new ideas. Probably the best-known example is that of the chemist Friedrich August von Kekulé whose name is synonymous with the structure of the benzene molecule. It is in fact a ring-shaped molecule which Kekulé claimed he discovered as a result of a vivid dream. Having been working on the problem of benzene and how its atoms might be arranged, Kekulé said that he dozed (or perhaps simply daydreamed) in front of the fire and had a vision in which chains of atoms writhed before his eyes in a snakelike motion. The crucial insight came when these atomic snakes began to form themselves into rings. 'One of the snakes,' he wrote, 'had seized hold of its own tail, and the form whirled mockingly before my eyes.'

Now there has been some dispute as to whether Kekulé was indeed dreaming at all, or whether he was just thinking hard about the problem. There has also been doubt raised as to whether the atoms in his imagination were in the form of snakes or simply writhed like snakes. The crucial point, though, is that the celebrated chemist did use his visual imagination to generate a new idea and that act of imagination had a strong analogical element to it.

Similarly, Albert Einstein is reported to have thought in signs and images which he combined in a kind of mental game analogous to the logical connections he was searching for in a scientific way. On reading Maxwell's theorem explaining light waves, Einstein is reported to have imagined himself riding through space, astride a light wave, and looking back at the wave next to him like a child on a merry-go-round. Many of us do something similar when we sketch out a rough geometric shape to represent say a social organization such as one finds in an office. Interrelationships can often be better understood in graphical form.

To what extent do creative people use visual or analogical thinking in this way? Reports of a subjective nature, even from eminent scientists, are notoriously anecdotal. People do not always recall past events accurately, nor are they necessarily adept at analysing their own creative processes. What is needed is some objective experiment in which people are asked to behave creatively and are given analogical help or not.

Fortunately such an experiment has been carried out by Dr Roy Dreistadt at New York's New School for Social Research. Dr Dreistadt set 80 male and female college students between the ages of 20 and 35 two problems: the Farm Problem and the Tree Planting Problem. Look at the illustrations below. In the farm problem the volunteers were

THE FARM PROBLEM   THE TREE PLANTING PROBLEM

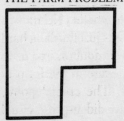

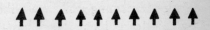

Plant 10 trees in 5 rows
with 4 trees in each row.

Divide the area of the
farm into four parts
which have the same
size and shape.

Source: The Journal of Psychology, 1969, p.71, article by Roy Dreistadt.

asked to divide the farm into four parts which have the same size and shape. In the tree planting problem the instruction was to plant ten trees in five rows with four trees in each row.

You may care to try your hand at these same problems yourself. Give yourself plenty of time. Twenty minutes would not be too long for each one.

Opposite are the correct answers. Incidentally these particular problems were chosen because, according to Dr Dreistadt, to solve them is to have exercised genuine creative thinking. No specialized knowledge is needed to work on them: they are by any standards difficult puzzles; and they are unusual. This means that a person is unlikely to have encountered them or others like them before, so that it is not

VISUAL AIDS FOR THE FARM PROBLEM

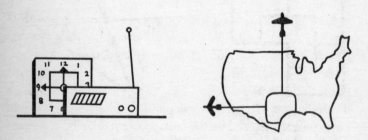

VISUAL AIDS FOR THE TREE PLANTING PROBLEM

just a question of transferring a learned technique to a different context. 'The experiment,' he writes, 'is thus a miniature model of the real thing.'

Dreistadt's subjects were arranged in groups. Some were given what he calls 'pictorial analogies' to help them, others were not. On p. 150 are examples of the visual aids provided for the two problems.

You can easily see the similarities between the correct solutions and the pictorial analogues, even though, of course, the subject-matter is quite different. The radio allows only a section of the clock face to show, the shape of which is

SOLUTION TO THE
FARM PROBLEM

SOLUTION TO THE TREE
PLANTING PROBLEM

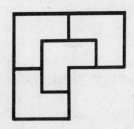

exactly what is needed for the farm problem. For the planting problem the cues are prominent five-pointed stars.

When the results were collated, with scores given for both total and partial solutions to the two problems, Dr Dreistadt found that people who had been given visual analogies performed better than those who had not. Thus, three people managed to solve the farm problem completely in the former group, compared to only one in the latter. Visual pictorial analogies, then, do seem to help people solve problems that draw on creative thinking. Dr Dreistadt's volunteers seemed to disregard the differences in subject-matter – between say a clown's hat and a forestry layout – and abstract the essential similarities in structure or form. Not only is the analogy used for solving the problem transferred to the problem, it is also transformed to make it relevant in a new context.

If we go back to the real world of scientific discovery, there is a striking comparison to be made. In the tree planting problem the solution involves using an analogy to put together the collection of parts – the trees – into a coherent whole – the planting pattern. Dreistadt likens this process to the work of the chemist John Newlands who anticipated the discovery of the Periodic Table by thinking of chemical elements like musical notes. When the elements are arranged in weight order every eighth element has properties that repeat, just as every eighth tone in music repeats in the normal scale. Newlands even called his discovery the Law of Octaves in Chemistry.

Self-discipline for all

In the course of this chapter we have touched on some important strategies for enhancing creativity, and seen how techniques can be acquired to rack up one's level of originality. But we conclude where we began, with the individual's own approach to the whole business of trying to do original and novel things, in whatever field. Creative people are by definition those who do not leap automatically at the first or easiest or obvious solution. They look around the problem and explore less immediate possibilities, however fanciful. This comes easier to some than to others, naturally. But we can all improve our performance by training – by telling ourselves not to accept the ordinary answer but to look for something exotic.

Try the exercise on p. 153. Interpret the drawings in the wildest way you can. Sure, number 5 looks like a rocket landing in front of a cactus but what else might it be? Number 28 looks very like your ink-stained school textbook. Any other thoughts? You can easily measure your creativeness here by playing the game with other people. If they laugh at your efforts you have succeeded in going beyond the banal to the genuinely creative. If they nod dully, try again.

WILD IMAGININGS

Source: Nicola de Carlo, *Psychological Games*, Facts on File Inc., 1984.

Summary

1 · Creative people may use rituals to help them to work. But these are not to be confused with genuine creative strategies.

2 · The flexible mind is not only nor even necessarily that of the diverger. Convergers too are creative.

3 · Likewise adaptors may be as creative as innovators.

4 · Motivation is of extreme importance to creative work.

5 · Brainstorming and group discussions are not as valuable as some people seem to think. But they can undoubtedly be useful if handled properly.

6 · Visualization and analogy are useful aids to creativity.

7 · It takes a lot of self-discipline not to jump to the obvious, non-creative solution. But practice helps.

8

EXPERT EDITORS

Genius consists in seeing what everyone has seen and thinking what no one has thought.

Albert Szent-Gyorgyi, discoverer of vitamin C

Genius . . . which means the transcendent capacity of taking trouble, first of all.

Thomas Carlyle

I judge one or two competitions and often you can see that (the amateur entries) are off target. They're nearly there, they may have a nice drawing, but the actual joke isn't focused, which does come with practice. Which makes one think that there's some muscle in the brain that actually gets sharpened just with usage.

Mel Calman

In 1947 the American psychologist L. M. Terman wrote: 'People like to believe that the genius as a rule is no better than the rest of us except in one particular. The facts are very different. Except in music and the arts, which draw heavily on specialized abilities, there are few persons who have achieved great eminence in one field without displaying more than average ability in one or more other fields.'

In this chapter, we will be following an alternative view – one characterized by the above quotations from Szent-Gyorgyi, Carlyle and Calman. It is this: ideas are two a penny. We all have them, in raw form, all the time. The trouble is, most of them are rubbish. We will argue that the person society considers to be creative is the one who can sort out the wheat of good ideas from the chaff of bad ones.

We will discuss ways in which this might be done. We will consider whether it is possible for anyone to improve his or her strike-rate of good ideas. In other words, whether anyone can be an expert editor.

Two a penny

'He hasn't got an idea in his head' is an insult often used by the 'creative' to dismiss those not so well endowed. In fact, every one of us is generating ideas continuously. Marvin Minsky, cognitive scientist and author of the book *The Society of Mind*, describes our everyday mental life thus:

> I don't think that there is a process of creativity in these people that is terribly different to ordinary people and my position is that people just don't have enough self-respect. We talk and we each make a new sentence that perhaps no one has ever said and we think that's all right because anybody can make a new sentence . . . but I think the average person is almost indistinguishable from the Mozart or Beethoven. An ordinary person

solves new problems every day just getting across the street with a crowd of people without hitting them, and making new sentences, and describing new experiences. It's just that our humanistic standards are such that we are always looking for heroes, but the amount of machinery it takes to do the sort of thing that everyone does all the time is immense. You know, a hundred billion brain cells are involved in talking and thinking and we take that for granted . . . We have so little self-confidence and we just look at our heroes and talk about them as being something beyond us and yet there's almost no difference.

Minsky's view, then is uncompromising. We all already exert massive amounts of mental effort just dealing with the world. The difference between those people we regard as geniuses and the rest of us is exceedingly small, perhaps no more than a froth on the surface of all the rest of our mental activity. The reason that these individuals stand out, according to Minsky, is that they have certain personality traits that drive them to process the products of their imaginations in a particular way:

If you just create, if you have a new idea and it's sort of off the wall, nobody will pay very much attention and they'll say not that you're creative, but that you're scatter-brained. And so the kind of artist or writer or that kind of creative person is someone who gets new ideas and then will work on it and perhaps think about it all the time. And you find that these geniuses or creative people are generally pretty intense. Even though they may not look so on the outside they're thinking all the time about how to pull something off.

Creativity as commonplace?

Minsky's analysis, then, seems to be turning us away from the view that creative ability resides in any exceptional capacities. Catharine Cox looked at the biographies of several hundred of the most eminent people in history. She concluded that they all had IQs above average, but she also made it clear that not everyone with a high IQ becomes a creative genius (see Chapter 3). Those that do, do so by 'persistence of motive and effort, confidence in their abilities, and great strength or force of character'. In this respect she and Marvin Minsky are fairly close. Genius is really pretty much run-of-the-mill, and it is application that matters, not any innate intellectual endowment.

Professor Robert Weisberg is also not persuaded by what he calls 'The Myth of Genius'.

Weisberg gives the example of Johann Sebastian Bach, which we mentioned in Chapter 1. It would take quite a lot of hard work today to unearth anybody who thinks that Bach's music is worthless. Yet for the best part of a century after his death, it produced no resonance in the public ear. Then, in the early 1800s, it began again to attract an audience. Now Bach is acknowledged as a monumental talent. Weisberg continues:

Here is the paradox: an artist whom we honour as a musician of unbelievable genius was ignored for seventy-five years after his death. If one believes that artistic genius includes the capacity to create in one's work elements that produce universal emotional responses in an audience, then how can Bach be classified as possessing musical genius when earlier generations dismissed him as having essentially no value? . . . It appears that the elements that serve at one time as the basis for acclamations of genius can at other times support the classification as a hack. Furthermore, whatever personal characteristics Bach possessed that determined how he wrote music, served at one and the same time to produce music of genius (i.e. the characteristics were those of a genius) and music of no value (i.e. the characteristics were those of a hack).

How to resolve this paradox? Weisberg introduces the idea of genius not as an inbuilt trait of the creator, but as something bestowed upon him or her by the audience. It is the appreciation of the audience that determines whether a work of art will have value. (Rather different standards apply in scientific creativity, but more of that later.)

Weisberg sums up: 'We are left with the conclusion that no special characteristics underlie artistic genius, and that the search for artistic genius is based on the notion that *being* a genius involves *possessing* genius.' (His italics.)

It seems to us that there is an alternative interpretation. Bach failed to achieve the recognition we now think he deserves because he was not aware of the needs of his audience. One thing that sets apart artists recognized as creative during their own lifetimes is that they have produced work which fits the mood of the time, or the specific needs of the audience.

One of the editing skills that anyone who wishes for instant recognition must acquire is that of throwing away ideas that the public is unready for, or unsympathetic to. At the same time, it is no good merely repeating what has already been successful. What is needed is, to quote the poet Gerard Manley Hopkins, 'Likeness tempered with difference'.

First, then, you must identify the likeness. Say you are trying to find a new way to open cans – a problem given by a client to the consulting engineer William J. J. Gordon when he was at the Arthur D. Little Company in the USA. Gordon had a group of other engineers and designers to work with him. But when he explained the problem to them, he deliberately did not use the term 'can opener'. His purpose was to avoid imposing any restrictions on the solutions they could come up with by preventing them from forming in their minds pictures of the conventional can openers found in any and every kitchen.

The likeness had been defined – come up with a way of opening cans. Then had come the difference – it had not necessarily to be what anyone might automatically conceive of as a 'can opener'. Gordon's group toyed with the task and aired such notions as the quasi-biological opener akin to the natural zipper of a banana. They came up with a variety of solutions, one of which eventually led to the ring pulls we now see on every soft drink and beer can. There is no doubt that the solution is technically speaking an excellent one – nowadays no one but a Boy Scout carries around a can opener on a key ring. But, more to the point so far as the manufacturer was concerned, it also seemed to appeal to the public – an idea that had hit its time. And a genuinely creative piece of marketing.

In fact, then, what the rest of the world considers to be the products of creative genius has a lot to do with us, and not so much to do with the person who created them. Except . . . what if a distinguishing mark of genius is the capacity to be sympathetic to the needs of an audience, either by chance, or quite deliberately?

It has been suggested (Chapter 3) that one of the character-istics of the creative process is a period of incubation. Here, the idea, wherever it might come from, is subjected to unconscious evaluation against the goals of the creative person. When, for instance, protracted conscious effort to solve a problem has been unsuccessful, then putting the problem out of your mind for a while can somehow bring out a solution. At first sight, this might appear to be the editorial process writ large, albeit not one carried out consciously.

The unconscious mind shuffles the possible solutions without the constraints imposed by conscious thinking.

In a paper published in 1976, Robert Olton and David Johnson, working at the University of California, set out to test whether incubation actually assisted in the solution of problems. Various psychological mechanisms have been proposed to explain the supposed existence of incubation. They range from the destruction of unproductive thinking patterns – breaking the mould, or extracting yourself from a thinking rut – to simple reduction of fatigue. Olton and Johnson devised an experiment to test all of these. At the outset, they both believed that incubation took place and was helpful. At the conclusion, they were not so sure.

The problem they chose was the 'Farm' problem, which as we saw in Chapter 7 had been used before to test for the value of visual analogy in problem-solving for creative thinkers. They gave this problem to 160 students at the University of California. Some of them worked continuously on it for thirty minutes or until they had solved it. Others were given ten minutes to try to solve the puzzle, and then given a break during which various things thought to encourage incubation happened to them. Some, for example, were placed in a dimly lit room. Classical music played softly. They were encouraged to relax. Others were given a different intellectual task – counting down by threes from 1187 was used. Still others were lectured on the dangers of falling into rigid thinking patterns, and so on.

To cut a long and complex story down to size, Olton and Johnson found no evidence that incubation existed. In fact they found that the people whose concentration had been interrupted did worse than those who had been left alone. In a long discussion of their results they pointed out a number of experimental difficulties which could account for their findings. None the less, they felt able to conclude that: 'One explanation of our negative findings is simply that incubation is unlikely (or, at best, marginal) under conditions that have typified most experimental studies of it, including the present one. "Real-life" accounts of the phenomenon describe a profoundly motivated person, a time period that often lasts for days or months, and a task that involves the use of a well-orchestrated, highly developed repertoire of cognitive skills and abilities appropriate to a specific body of knowledge.'

If it is not unconscious incubation, then, what might be the driving force of creation? The answer might lie in conscious, but protracted, editing. How might this work?

The editor in action

We have all been faced with problems that appear to have a number of possible solutions. Sometimes we will find good ones, sometimes bad, but it is rare for them simply to pop unbidden into our minds. Usually the right answer is the result of a conscious, logical, thinking process. Consider the following problem. You are presented with a candle, a book of matches, and a box of drawing pins, and instructed to attach the candle to a wooden door in such a way that it provides enough light to read by. This problem was originated by Karl Dunckner over 50 years ago, and has provided much fun for psychologists ever since.

It appears that there are two possible solutions. Use a drawing pin to fix the candle to the door. Or melt some wax and use it as glue. But there is another way. Empty all the drawing pins out of the box. Pin the box to the door. Put the candle in the box. This is obviously the best solution. No wax drips on the floor. The candle is unlikely to drop out of the box. It can be positioned to cast light in the desired direction.

How did this solution emerge? Not, it seems, from the unconscious. Studies of people asked to solve this problem have shown that they work through definite chains of reason-

THE CANDLE PROBLEM

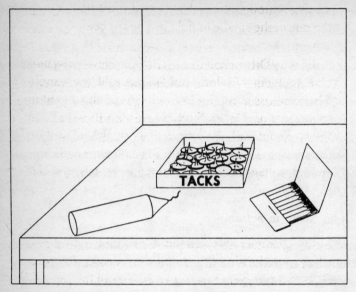

Source: Robert W. Weisberg, *Creativity – Genius and Other Myths*, W. H.
Freeman, 1986.

ing. What have been called 'verbal protocols' illustrate the
point. Volunteers are asked to talk aloud about the thoughts
that go through their minds as they try to solve the problem.
The supposition is that verbalizing will not change the way
the thinking process works – this seems to be true. Robert
Weisberg quotes from three protocols obtained from people
who were *thinking* about the problem, but who did not have
physical access to the materials.

Subject 1: 'Candle has to burn straight, so if I took a nail
and put it through the candle . . . (ten seconds) . . . if I
took several nails and made a row and put the candle on
that. If I took the nails out of the box, nailed the box to
the wall . . . '

Subject 2: 'Put a nail into the candle so it supports the

candle, so as the candle burns it won't fall. But the nail won't go through the candle, so put some nails around the side of the candle to hold it. Use the box . . . '

Subject 3: 'Drive a nail through the candle – a long nail. One problem – a long nail might split the candle. Therefore use a thin nail. You might be able to put up some nails next to each other and burn the candle on them, or put nails into the wall along the sides of the candle . . . There don't seem to be enough nails large enough so you could . . . Another way, take the box, etc. . . . '

What these protocols show is that the solution is not arrived at as a bolt from the blue. It is the result of a conscious process. The process takes into account knowledge of the capabilities of the materials on offer – the length of the drawing pins, the stickiness and strength of candle wax as a glue, the weight and durability of candles, the carrying capabilities of boxes. It then operates on them to generate a number of possible solutions. This is done consciously and linearly. Solutions are tested against the demands of the problem. When they are found wanting they are rejected, and another one sought. When a solution is found that meets all the requirements of the problem – or at least as few as the problem-solver is prepared to put up with – it is accepted.

This appears to be fine for the sort of relatively low-level problem-solving shown here. But how might it work for more complex problems?

In the case of science it is relatively easy to see how editing fits. In fact, science is often perceived as a process of linear, rational logic. But it appears that scientists are by no means immune to the feeling that they have suddenly received a flash of inspiration. Richard Feynman, probably the most accomplished physicist in modern times, tells the story of how, at one point in his distinguished career, he lost interest in doing physics. All the fun had gone out of it for him, so he decided that all he would do it for *was* fun – he would only work on the problems that he found entertaining.

One day he happened to walk into the cafeteria at Cornell University: 'Some guy, fooling around, throws a plate in the air. As the plate went up in the air I saw it wobble, and I noticed the red medallion of Cornell on the plate going around. It was pretty obvious to me that the medallion went around faster than the wobbling. I had nothing to do, so I start to figure out the motion of the rotating plates. I discover that when the angle is very slight, the medallion rotates twice as fast as the wobble rate – two to one. It came out of a complicated equation! Then I thought, "Is there some way I can see in a more fundamental way, by looking at the forces or the dynamics, why it's two to one?" '

Sure enough, Feynman found the solution. Great for plates, perhaps, but useless for anything else. In fact, Feynman went on to 'work on the equations of wobbles. Then I thought about how electron orbits start to move in relativity. Then there's the Dirac equation in electro-dynamics. And then quantum electrodynamics. And before I knew it (it was a very short time) I was "playing" – working, really – with the same old problem . . . It was effortless. It was easy to play with these things. It was like uncorking a bottle: everything flowed out effortlessly. There was no importance to what I was doing, but ultimately there was. The diagrams and the whole business that I got the Nobel Prize for came from that piddling around with the wobbling plate.' (*Surely You're Joking, Mr Feynman!*)

On the face of it, Feynman's story fits the inspirational model of scientific discovery. Out of a few wobbling plates comes profound insight into the fundamental workings of the universe. But it may be that the emphasis is wrong. That the important part of Feynman's story is not the fact that he was spurred by a wobble, but that he had in his mind a file of relevant information – the Dirac equation, quantum electrodynamics, and so on – and the logical faculties to make sense of it. Clearly, he had to work out whether his answer to the problem was satisfactory. And here editing has to come into play.

For there is one factor that sets scientific creativity apart from other kinds – its products have to fit the way the world works. It is no good having the most beautiful theory in the world if it cannot explain why things happen around us in the ways that they do. There must therefore be a process of testing the idea – what Jacques Hadamard in his study of mathematical creativity called step 4: verification, exposition, and utilization of the results (see Chapter 3). It can be easy for scientists themselves to mistake the importance of this process. The great mathematician Paul Dirac, for instance, said that he was principally motivated by the search for beauty in his formulae. But this beauty was not purely aesthetic. Dirac's formulae also 'work', in that they chime with what we know about the world. Indeed, his status as an original thinker in mathematics would be in serious doubt if his beautiful creations turned out to be worthless. Similarly, when Watson and Crick unravelled the structure of DNA they found a double helix of elegance and simplicity: but the important thing is that it worked. It explained how genetic material could manufacture proteins. In every sense of the expression, it is the secret of life.

But Watson and Crick had laboured long and hard to get to the double helix. Many other structures, some equally appealing, had been discarded – edited out of their sphere of activity – because they did not fit the evidence. Richard Feynman has characterized this part of science as 'all you have to do is to imagine what's there'. It still seems like pretty hard work.

It may be, then, that the nature of science makes it a natural home for editing as a creative process. But it is much harder to see how it can operate in the arts. How does a painter edit his work, for instance? In the formative stages, he or she will obviously edit the basic idea. From simply deciding what to paint to subtler questions of colour and technique, competing ideas will be tested against the artist's conception and accepted or discarded.

One painting which has undergone a great deal of analysis in this fashion is Pablo Picasso's *Guernica*. Painted by Picasso to commemorate the bombing of the town of Guernica during the Spanish Civil War, it vies for the title of 'best-known painting in the world' with the *Mona Lisa*. Not only is it striking in its execution, it also has an immense emotional impact. The horrors of war are communicated with extreme power.

Guernica contains nine major visual metaphors (see illustration section). The sun is reduced to a light bulb at the top edge of the painting. A bird is flying towards it. In the centre is a horse in a rictus of suffering. In the top right a woman falls helplessly. Another woman peers from a window. A stylized bull stands over a third woman. She holds a dead child, and appears to be weeping. A fourth woman is striding from the bottom right of the canvas towards the centre. At bottom left lies a dead soldier, holding a broken sword.

One reason for the painting's popularity among those interested in creativity, apart from its undoubted value as a work of the highest creativity, is that Picasso kept all of his preparatory work. These versions make it plain that Picasso toyed with and rejected a number of compositions before reaching the final work. In other words, he edited.

There are several things to note about the artist's preliminary sketches (see the illustration section). Many of them bear very little relation to the finished painting. Major characters are absent. The placing of the elements within the frame is very different. But equally important, the sketches mostly bear little relation to each other. It is not a matter of starting with a fixed concept of what the final picture will look like. Rather, it appears that Picasso cast about extensively in his visual vocabulary until he found something that met his vision. All his other attempts were rejected.

Robert Weisberg has summarized Picasso's approach to painting thus:

> The evidence for detailed critical analysis is visible in Picasso's work, both before the mural was begun, and while it was being painted. Several possibilities for the general composition of the mural were considered before Picasso began to paint, and the composition underwent further changes while he painted. Likewise, specific aspects of the characters were considered again and again in preliminary work and then modified still further as the painting progressed . . . one gets the feeling that Picasso is very hard to satisfy and always ready to try once more to get some small detail a little better.

This sounds like nothing more nor less than the editorial process in action. Set a goal, in this case a painting depicting the horrors of war. Consider the materials and techniques available to you. Formulate a solution. Test it against your goal. If it works, accept it. If it does not, reject it and start again, either from scratch, or by modifying your previous attempt.

In this context, Carlyle's comment – 'Genius . . . means the transcendent capacity of taking trouble, first of all' – takes on some force. The work of genius, the creative work, is the result of a painstaking process of testing the work in progress against the desired goal.

A further question is then raised. How does work become

complete? At what point does the creator say, 'Enough is enough, that's as close as I'm going to get to perfection'? The answer varies from case to case. Again, in science, an end-point is usually defined once the problem to be solved has been formulated. The solution either works or it doesn't.

In the arts, it appears to depend on the personality of the artist. The cartoonist Mel Calman owns to an almost physical sense of separation when asked to part with one of his creations: 'You kind of surrender it. There's this theory that a lot of people don't finish things. I mean I've had trouble with that, because you're reluctant to get rid of them because when they're finished they're no longer your children, and people can say, "Huh, don't think much of that." I mean, if you see something printed, it's not as good as it was inside your head.'

It seems that, as in everything else to do with creating, you have to work at knowing when to stop.

The expert editor

Where then stands the expert editor? Are we now in a position to define the skills needed to evaluate the worth of ideas? So far, several elements have emerged.

Clearly, it is important to have some goal in mind, even if it is only expressed in a nebulous form. In problem-solving, the end-point is usually obvious – it is something that solves the problem. In artistic pursuits it can be more unfocused. The painter, for instance, will generally not have in mind the exact form of the final composition when he or she sets pencil to paper. But what will be in mind is some strong idea of what the painting is meant to express. In science we find a combination of the two. There is a problem to be solved, but scientists are loth to accept a solution that is ugly. They prefer their findings – particularly mathematical formulations of them – to have beauty.

Here lies the first important element of creative editing. Do not make do with the easy solution. In the trivial case of the candle problem we considered above, there were obvious solutions. They required little in the way of creative ability. But there was also a much better way to secure the candle to the door. To find it required that the easy solutions were not taken as the only ones. The creative people who found the best solution were prepared to work just that little bit harder to find something novel and better.

In the same way, what we consider to be the creative artist is the one who is not prepared to take the easy options of creation. We do not respect the composer whose music sounds like that of a hundred others. He has found a solution almost anyone else possessed of the basic technical vocabulary could have found. On the contrary, we reserve our appreciation for those who reject the easy route, and instead expend the effort needed to come up with something fresh.

The second element is that the expert editor must have a strong, well-defined and coherent picture of the context in which he or she makes a judgement. We have seen that creative people recognize the importance of knowledge. They are all aware of the need to know not only what others in the same field have done, but also what creative people in other spheres have accomplished. From this knowledge spring the roots of their own work. The expert editor must spend time acquiring a knowledge base by extensive study. Many people must have had an idea for a novel about one man's quest for a great white whale. Sadly, it has already been done. There are no short cuts to acquiring this attribute. Creative people, to quote David Ogilvy, have an insatiable curiosity about the world around them. They indulge this curiosity. They thereby acquire more knowledge. Their creative abilities are also thereby increased.

There is another component to being aware of the context. It is being aware of public taste. No matter what area of creativity you wish to operate in, it is important to make sure that the products of your efforts strike some chord in the public mind. That is, unless your ambition is to die unrecognized and be rediscovered by posterity. But as Groucho Marx said: 'What's posterity ever done for me?'

This awareness takes many forms. It can be generated by systematic study. Terence Conran has already said that to be a successful designer it is necessary to know what people wear, what music they listen to, what they eat, where they go on holiday, and so on. Other creative people have approached their work in an equally calculating fashion. Glossy best-sellers set in Hollywood, or swashbuckling bodice-rippers clearly have elements of a formula to them. To write one successfully, the author must be aware of the elements of the formula. He or she must also be prepared to put in a great deal of hard work, as every publisher knows. We're a long way from the machine-made pulp cranked out in George Orwell's *1984*.

It is also necessary to be ready to grasp chance happenings, to direct your mental antennae towards every chance happening in case it may be of value. The cartoonist James Thurber is supposed to have started a drawing of two seals sitting on a rock. When it was almost finished, the rock had started to look like a bed. So he made it into a bed and put two people in it. The final element in the drawing was the caption. One is saying to the other: 'Have it your way – you heard a seal bark.' On the face of it, pure serendipity. But notice that most people would have seen two seals sitting on a rock. Thurber was prepared to reject the obvious, and allow, indeed direct, his thoughts on to a better, more creative use of his luck. Fortune does indeed favour the prepared mind.

Practical editing

So far, we have examined the theory of creative editing. Now comes the practical. The sculptor Jonathan Kenworthy was recently commissioned to create a statue to stand outside 20, Canon Street, opposite St Paul's Cathedral in the City of London. Kenworthy is particularly known for his studies of Africa, both its people and its wildlife. He chose as his subject a leopard. Here is how he came to that decision.

> Several years ago, when I was driving in London, my route took me past a number of public statues.
>
> It struck me at the time that the formalised way the statues were displayed on high granite plinths tended to give them an austere character and, certainly for my taste, made some fine sculpture unapproachable in a municipal sort of way.
>
> I wondered if it might be possible to elevate the sculpture to a suitable height by another method. Perhaps if the plinth was incorporated as a part of the sculpture, so that the viewer's eye was led from ground level to the main features of the piece in a natural flowing way.

As the sculpture began to crystallise in his mind, Kenworthy started a series of drawings to test out his ideas. He kept them all. In the illustration section you will find seven. Your task is to apply your critical faculties and put yourself inside the head of the sculptor. As you follow his description below of the genesis of the famous leopard sculpture, try to see how and why Kenworthy came to direct his energies as he did. Don't try to rush it. Weigh the possibilities carefully. After all, the sculptor himself took a long time to decide. And his decision was built upon a lifetime's accumulated aesthetic – and practical – experience.

Back in my studio I sifted through drawings and found a sketch I had made of a leopard in the Serengeti. The cat was poised on the craggy remains of a tree that had been struck by lightning [Fig 1]. It was alert, watching the gazelles out on the plains and I thought this concept would serve as a starting point for my work.

At this stage I like to work round an idea by developing all the likely permutations of a theme I can envisage. In this case I began by simply drawing a leopard on a tree [Fig 2].

Then I went on safari in the Serengeti again and felt it would be exciting to include the Kopjes, the rocks that rise up dramatically out of the grasslands and are used by the predators as cover and towers from which they can survey the passing herds.

For the moment, I abandoned the tree and started working with the leopard set on an outcrop of rocks [Fig 3].

Moulded through the aeons by the elements, the granite Kopjes are fascinating shapes and I made drawings of them with and without leopards [Figs 4a and 4b]. In the end I refined my choice to a large single rock with a cluster of smaller boulders round its base [Fig 5]. I made a sketch model and then I wondered if the bulk of the rock might overpower the leopard.

I took away the rock and brought back the tree – but now it was surrounded at its base by rocks [Fig 6].

It began to look as if I had found the strongest permutation. The curve of the tree made it almost like a spring, ready to propel the leopard forward, and the boulders now introduced around the base formed an aesthetic counterbalance to the leopard at the top of the tree.

The shape and pitch of the boulders evolved as I made the next sketch model and by the time it was finished I felt ready to start on the full-sized sculpture.

I set up the armature and worked for a year and a half to complete the bronze.

Although the main features of the twelve-foot sculpture were decided in the drawings and sketch models, much creative work of a different sort still lay ahead of me. The critical forms and balances which give the final sculpture its character could only be evolved as the large model was actually made.

The evolution of an idea is seldom straightforward for me. The Leopard was created in one concentrated period, but I normally develop my thoughts by working on a series of sculptures, with as many as fifteen models taking shape in the studio during one work cycle. This allows me time to give each piece consideration, and a series of this nature can take up to six years to complete.

Summary

1 · One of the main things that sets creative people apart is their judgement of the worth of their ideas. They must be prepared to reject the duds ruthlessly.

2 · To judge, they must be prepared to work – it is no good accepting the easy solution to a creative problem.

3 · They must have knowledge of other work in the same area, and in other separate, but potentially relevant areas.

4 · They also must have a well-developed sense of the times they live in. In other words, a sensitivity to public taste.

5 · They must develop the habit of analysing the work of other creative people, of always asking: 'Why did he do it that way?'

9

CREATIVITY IN ACTION:
Doing it Yourself

The creative editorial skills that we saw in action in the last chapter can only be cultivated through practice. It is no more possible to think creatively without preparing yourself through training than it is to run a marathon. In fact the successful athlete and the creative thinker have a lot in common. Both need a lot of dedication to push themselves on when there is something more passive and enticing to do. Both are essentially lonely occupations. No one else can do it for them. And both offer themselves up for some kind of test of performance. There are unfortunately no gymnasia devoted to mental calisthenics. But below are a few hints on self-preparation.

Limbering up: an imaginative assignment

Imagine that you are serving on a jury in a murder trial, trying to make sense of the evidence that has been prepared. Two points have, in the course of the hearing, been established without a shadow of a doubt:

1. That the victim was stabbed to death in a cinema during the afternoon showing of *Bambi*.
2. That the suspect was on an express train to Edinburgh when the murder occurred.

What conclusion would you draw from this data?

This is the problem posed by Dr Philip Johnson-Laird of the Applied Psychology Unit in Cambridge to demonstrate that, even in the coolly reasonable atmosphere of the court-room a certain amount of creative thinking can be invaluable.

As you mull over the riddle of 'The *Bambi* Case', you might come up with a few obvious suggestions: that the suspect is innocent, for example. In the course of an experiment with hundreds of volunteers, this is what Dr Johnson-Laird found that most people thought. However, reject that possibility yourself for the moment and try to conceive of another. You might then think that there was a cinema on the London to Edinburgh express train. This is conceivable but not in fact the case. Try again. Did the suspect have an accomplice? This was another thought to occur to the subjects in the Cambridge experiment. But no accomplice was hinted at in any of the evidence. How then might a murderer have accomplished his wicked ends? A spring-loaded knife on the seat perhaps? A knife suspended in a block of ice above the victim's seat? Even perhaps a radio-controlled robot?

There is in fact another fiendishly clever method that a murderer might use. We shall come to it later. Meanwhile try to discard the normal, everyday reasoning that we all tend to fall into so rapidly. It is tempting to imagine a scenario in which the train and the cinema are brought together spatially to become one and the same place. Believing that the man in the dock might be innocent, for example, derives from the automatic and logical inference that to be the murderer our suspect would have to be, like the victim, in the cinema while also being on the train. Impossible.

It is only when we break out of the closed formal rules that govern our everyday reasoning that we succeed in coming up with other, valid scenarios, such as the use of a suspended knife or the services of an obliging robot. But these have inbuilt difficulties. They are prone to fail or misfire or to some other mechanical disruption.

By persisting, though, with the general concept of 'killing-at-a-distance' and adding to it a further idea – that the suspect killed himself – you can juxtapose the two ideas to come up with other, more valid scenarios. Of several hundred people given this problem, by the way, Dr Johnson-Laird only found two that spontaneously came up with a suggestion that seemed to fit the bill. The suspect gave the victim a post-hypnotic suggestion to stab himself during a certain climactic scene in the film. Ingenious, but it is not the only possibility. Undoubtedly Conan Doyle or Agatha Christie, were they alive to be asked, would be able to come up with one or two more. Can you think of any other likely scenarios by building on the killing-at-a-distance framework?

An aid to artistic creativity: the prolific potato

Creativity is a way of using one's internal resources. Everyone has these resources, therefore everyone is in some degree creative. Even if you accept that basic assumption you may baulk at the thought that this applies to all forms of creative activity: that everyone has the wherewithal to be creative in any field. Or at least more creative than they are now.

If you were one of those people who, during school art classes, spent most of the time staring morosely at a still-life arrangement, and even more sadly at your attempts to capture this on paper, you might well be sceptical. How can someone with 'no talent for painting', as it might have said on your end-of-term report, even assume any artistic skill? How could a person with a so-called 'tin ear' hope to create anything of a musical nature? Surely, the artistically creative person is one who has always made beautiful things?

Not so. The artistic shortcomings of the apparently non-creative individual may be less severe than he or she might imagine. In a strangely powerful article with the evocative title 'The Potato Print as Talent Amplifier' the psychologist Dr John Clark of Manchester University reminds us that most people have far more artistic taste than artistic talent (in the sense of being able to generate works of art). This is why amateur painters or sculptors often feel very frustrated, producing technically inadequate works that fail to express what they have in heart and mind.

The trouble lies often in the sheer quantity, or rather lack of quantity, of work produced. 'Talentless' people take a long time to produce anything: although they labour long and hard they know the final outcome is probably doomed because they sense their own slide into ineptitude. If only they could generate lots of fresh ideas with the carefree abandon and boldness that lies locked up, trapped in their heads.

Here is where the humble potato comes in, as a 'talent amplifier'. You can, says Dr Clark, use the potato to make prints that are far more subtle and rewarding in their effects than the sort of thing you turned out during your primary school days. The potato is cut in half and the flat cut surface used for printing.

PROLIFIC POTATOES

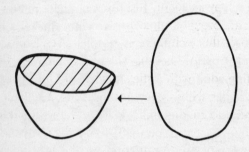

CUTTING THE TALENT AMPLIFYING POTATO

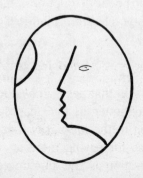

Paint the surface black and blot it on newspaper. This will help to show up your cuts. Using a small-bladed penknife, cut designs such as the one below a couple of millimetres deep. Then apply acrylic paint with a brush to the surface and press it down on a plain white filing card. Put on more, different-coloured paints and make more prints, dozens, scores, even a hundred or more. Keep on printing. When you have amassed a large stack, keep looking at the prints over the next few days, selecting only those that you really like and discarding the rest (along with the potato). Be ruthless with what you reject. 'Print with abandon but select with care,' says Dr Clark. Eventually you will end up with a half-dozen or so that really appeal to you, produced by a combination of skill and happy accident. Just the way many more complex creations are brought into being.

Although the technique is simple, even childish, it is deceptively useful because it does provide the self-deprecating adult with a slick mechanism for liberating the talent that lies within everyone. Results are quick, always totally unique to the individual, and the final selection enables one to exercise personal taste – the ultimate test-bed for any work of art. A variation on the talent amplifying potato is the prolific computer. One can program domestic micro computers to generate particular word combinations – from expletives to poetic descriptions. Again, you can choose the outcomes you prefer from a long list of possibles.

'You are a camera . . . ': looking as lubrication

One important skill that needs to be courted by the would-be creative practitioner, is that of observation. Rosemary Gaymer, writing in the *Journal of Creative Behavior*, puts forward the case for paying more attention to good old-fashioned observation as 'the spiralling, braided and multi-coloured element winding through the field of creativity'.

We can, she argues, teach ourselves to observe better and thereby fuel our creative efforts by providing ourselves with a richer perceptual input. Like a camera, we can record better if we are correctly focused on what is around us. And if we are observing well we do so actively, aware and attentive to available inputs.

This helps creativity in several ways. First, good observation makes us more sensitive to problems that might be around needing solution. By observing, for example, the body language of others we can gain insights into submerged challenges; picking out anomalies, perhaps, and noticing what is out of line. Creative people do not only solve problems. They also find problems to be solved.

Secondly, good observation is the basis of competent fact-finding and idea finding. The keener and faster our powers of observation, the more likely we are to spot useful concepts and see them in juxtaposition or conjunction with others. The more ideas we are attuned to the more we can manipulate them in valuable ways. When a poet concocts a surprising metaphor or simile, or a painter reveals what is familiar in a novel way, it is because they have access to a rich internal data bank. They exploit possibilities mentally by scanning what has been stored through experience. Observation is their antenna on to the outside world.

Be a better camera!

How can we improve our all-important observational powers? Rosemary Gaymer offers four strategies for enhancing this 'most useful of skills'.

METHOD 1

· Close the eyes, and keep them closed during this exercise.
· *Gently* put the palms of your hands over your closed eyes so that you feel the contact, but *do not* put any pressure on your eyeballs. Relax.

· *Think* of an object – anything – anyplace.

· *Visualize* the object *as a whole* . . . hold it still in your mind for a few moments.

· Now *visualize* that object's elements and aspects . . . look 'for' each in turn . . . look for details, different angles, colors and *describe* them to yourself or someone else.

· *Manipulate* the object in your mind: *watch* it revolve in every direction and observe it from different angles.

· *Be conscious of your eye movement* . . . how they move in response to your thoughts and mental imaging.

Method 2

· *Imagine yourself at home* or in another room if you are home while reading this; if you are not home, go there mentally.

· Keeping your *eyes shut*, actively look 'for' and visualize . . .

the layout of the room,

the furniture,

objects on tables or shelves,

walls, pictures and hangings,

the view from the window.

Seek as much detail as possible.

· Again, consciously *feel* how your eyes move, even when you focus on minute details. If you find it difficult to feel that movement, mentally 'zoom in' on whatever you are examining, so your mind's eye has a larger target to search for details.

(If, when you start doing these exercises, you find your eyes becoming tense, try the following:

Keep your eyes shut but don't palm them. *Relax.* Look straight up slowly, as far as you can without moving your head; then lower your eyes straight down as far as possible. Move your eyes smoothly, without straining.

Sweep your eyes from side to side as far as they will go,

slowly and smoothly. Keep them level and try to 'track round the equator' of your eyeballs.

Sweep your eyes obliquely, from the upper left to lower right corners, and from upper right to lower left, and reverse, in the same slow gentle manner.

Looking straight ahead – *eyes still closed* – relax your eyes as much as possible by thinking of a color until you can see it, then let it develop into any other color and enjoy the restfulness.)

Both accurate observation and recall are closely linked to description, and good retention of observation often depends on description to etch it into memory. The description might be:

silent – running the observation through your mind, consciously thinking each point;

spoken – to yourself or someone else;

written – in jot-form to speed the process, in longhand, shorthand or any form of symbolic representation;

sketched – either a picture of whatever was observed or a diagrammatic illustration of the concepts.

METHOD 3

· *Choose anything* available (stamp, coin, book, record or cassette cover, photograph, section of a map, pattern on fabric or wallpaper, item of clothing, item on a desk).

· *Observe it for a set time*, say, two minutes to start with. Look at nothing else. Don't speak or write anything. Don't even think of words to describe it. Just let your eyes follow the lines, intersects, colors, proportions or various different elements and textures.

· Then turn away and, *without looking*, record as much detail as possible, either spoken, written or sketched.

· When you can think of nothing more, *compare your* description with the original.

· *Take note* of what aspects you omitted . . . and *keep your notes*.

As you practise this *over a period of time, analyse aspects that were omitted*. Is there a common denominator among them? Does your recall or vision wander when confronted by certain colors, patterns, shapes, *types* of details (e.g., straight lines or curved lines; asymmetrical or symmetrical patterns), intersect points or relative sizes? What messages do you receive from the analysis? Maybe the omissions are random, but you might discover a hole in your attention through which valuable observations can slip. This can be a focal point for practice until either the hole is closed or you have found a way to compensate for it.

METHOD 4

· *Practise throwing quick glances at things*, recording what you have observed (drawn, written, spoken), then quickly checking your accuracy. You might use such targets as:

   licence plates on cars:
   the layout of an advertisement;
   the design of a poster;
   the pattern of thumb-tacks on a bulletin board;
   the shape and color distribution details of birds, insects or flowers;
   the order and colors of books on a shelf;
   the seating arrangement in a conference room or the ceiling details in an auditorium.

The subject matter is of no importance. What is important is that you keep on practising, turning it into a game and improving your skill. *Feedback about accuracy* of observation is essential if there is to be improvement.

Source: *The Journal of Creative Behavior*, vol. 19, no. 1, 1985, article by Rosemary Gaymer.

Remedial measures: removing creative blocks

If creative skills can to a large extent be learned, so too can techniques for maintaining a flow of novel ideas when they appear to be drying up. At the Manchester Business School, Les Jones has studied the common barriers to effective problem-solving in particular, though his recommended solutions might well be applied to any other area of creative endeavour.

Les Jones categorizes thinking blocks in four ways. First there are what he terms 'Strategic Barriers'. These affect the way in which we tackle problems, and the most obvious is habit. We tend to stick to our well-used, tried-and-tested ways of tackling problems even though they may not be appropriate. To overcome this one needs to be totally honest with oneself; at the risk of having to discard habits that may stretch back many years.

Another strategic block lies in our tendency to censor ideas before giving them a chance to flower, to strangle at birth a brainchild that could show enormous promise. If this kind of block occurs, the technique is to try to separate idea generation from evaluation. Suppose, for example, you are trying to devise new ways of rearranging the furniture or perhaps reorganizing the office administration. Do not reject any idea at first blush, simply because it seems impracticable or expensive or downright silly. Make a list or draw up various plans and sketches as the ideas come to you. When that part of the creative process is over, you can then calmly begin to pick through them one by one, weighing their merits. 'You will be surprised,' writes Dr Jones, 'how many of the unlikely ideas prove to be useful in themselves or stimulate other good ideas.' Moreover, by having all your ideas stretched out before you, you might make some creative connections between different items.

The second barrier to creativity is one of perspective, founded on our particular values, attitudes and beliefs. We are all to some extent trapped within the narrow confines of our own value systems. We hold beliefs about society, politics, religions, human relationships and so on that have become part of the essential 'Us' over many years. As the psychologist Dr David Taylor puts it: 'Belief or attitudes may bias the reasoning process, perhaps at an unconscious level . . . much of what we call rational thinking is not nearly as rational as we would like to think.' However, a difficult problem might well arise where one creative solution clashes directly with our personal values. We might find it therefore unacceptable.

Suppose, for example, you were the owner of a small firm that you had built up over the years with the aid of long-serving and loyal employees. You fall on hard times and need to rethink your business completely. One solution that could make excellent commercial sense is to throw open the ownership of the company to some of your employees, if not all of them – a kind of workers' co-operative. Because you have for so long maintained the classic worker/manager relationship you might be tempted to reject that reform out of hand. Yet it could save the business.

Thirdly there are the 'Perceptual Barriers' to creative thinking. Our brains fail to take in or act upon many of the cues we get from our environment because at the time they seem unimportant. Or we may think that we are taking every factor into account when invariably we are working on quite limited data. A study of the thinking process of stockbrokers showed that they need to consider as many as ten or twelve different characteristics when evaluating stocks and shares. Indeed they believe that they do use all this information when making their buying and selling decisions. In reality, though, their choices are determined by only five or six characteristics. When faced with that fact the stockbrokers themselves were unable even to say which characteristics these were.

In a similar vein we might do badly in an examination because we failed to read the question carefully. Or we might formulate a judgement about a person based exclusively on what he or she says using the spoken word, without taking into account the rich variety of non-verbal cues being generated. As a general rule we can improve our performance on creative thinking tasks by slowing down, listening and reading more carefully, and checking with ourselves that we have taken in and understood precisely what the problem is that we are tackling. In addition there is a fairly narrow band of what psychologists call 'Arousal', both physical and emotional, in which we can think clearly. If we are too charged up, on the verge of panic or too cool to the point of sleepiness, we are unlikely to perform particularly well.

The final category of creative blocks is the 'Self-Image Barrier'. This is particularly relevant, not so much to coming up with good ideas but in seeing them through, often by persuading others of their value. Here it pays to be self-assertive. If you have what you think is a good idea, air it. Conversely, if someone comes to you with an 'inspired thought' and you have misgivings about it, give expression to those as well. This does not mean that the creative person has to be wildly aggressive. But it does mean that you should be prepared to stand up your ideas for scrutiny. If they fail to match the demands put upon them, then perhaps they were not such good ideas after all.

This kind of barrier has particular relevance to novel products and inventions, where too much reticence may stifle the development of an idea that could turn out to initiate a revolution. In 1945 a gifted inventor at the Raytheon factory in Massachusetts called Percy Spencer had what seemed like a crazy idea. He was working on the magnetron, the device at the heart of the then novel radar system, when he realized that the radiation it emitted could have a culinary use. He hung a pork chop in front of the machine – and produced the first microwave meal in history. However it was decades before the microwave oven industry began to take off commercially. Ironically it was the Japanese who capitalized on the invention. When a Japanese firm started to manufacture magnetrons it was forbidden under the peace treaty to undertake military contracts. Therefore it concentrated on peaceful uses of microwave technology: now Japan leads the world in microwave oven sales.

One of the reasons why Japan has succeeded so brilliantly in technology-based industry is that new ideas do not sink under a poor self-image. By doggedly persisting in the apparently laughable notion that there was money to be made from the sales of pocket-sized tape recorders that do not record, the inventors of the Walkman stereo cassette player demonstrated that creativity is not just a matter of having ideas. It may also mean promoting them in the face of considerable opposition and scepticism. Creative fortune favours the bold.

Summary

1 · Set about enhancing your creativity as an athlete improves performance, bit by bit over time, with constant practice.

2 · Aim initially to enhance the sheer quantity of your output. Quality comes later.

3 · Train yourself to be more observant. Many problems requiring creativity evaporate when you take in the whole picture. Observation is your link with a rich pool of ideas and images.

4 · Creative blocks can be identified and analysed. They can often also be removed.

10

THE CREATIVE FUTURE:
A Matter of Training

We are all creative.
> *Arthur VanGundy, University of Oklahoma*

'All is flux, nothing stays still,' wrote the Greek philosopher Heraclitus in the sixth century BC. For the singer Bob Dylan, two-and-a-half millennia later, it was equally true that 'Times they are a-changing'. In the broadest sweep of a cosmic perspective or on the microscopic scale of atoms and molecules, nothing remains static. Look up at a still, cloudless sky at one moment. Then look again five minutes later and something will have happened. However imperceptible, there will have been change. Talk to someone on one day and then again the following day, and both of you will have become different people in the meantime. You can never pick up precisely where you left off. We all, constantly, have to adapt to a fresh tableau.

For this reason one can see the logic in the argument that human beings as a matter of course, in the conduct of their everyday lives, are permanently engaged in creative thinking. It is inevitable. Because no two experiences are ever identical we have to modify our responses to meet the demands of the unique present. No two responses will ever be alike because no two situations are the same. It could be argued, then, that we are all responding creatively to our environment all the time: that creativity is perfectly normal. Indeed – to take this to the logical extreme – we could not function properly by being un-creative.

Increasingly, as we have seen in earlier chapters, this view is being endorsed by researchers into the creative process. Professor Marvin Minsky of MIT, for example, taking up the notion of adapting to change, reckons that what generally pass for 'acts of creation' are but the tip of an enormous iceberg – we notice only the conspicuous, brilliant or socially valued part. Underneath lies vastly more. In crossing a road or cutting down a rose bush, Minsky says, we are employing a multitude of adaptive skills. The kind of activity that constitutes 'creativity' as the term is normally used represents but a noticeable fraction above this baseline.

Professor Arthur VanGundy of the Department of Human Relations, University of Oklahoma, is another believer in the universality of creativity: 'To be human is to be creative,' he writes. 'The trick is to use our innate and acquired creativity to help us solve our major problems.' To capitalize, though, on the freely available resource we call creativity we have to recognize that we possess that asset in the first place. And the best way to do that is to exercise and develop it, like any other skill or aptitude. We have, in short, to put creativity where it belongs – in the classroom.

A creative curriculum

There was a time, and not very long ago at that, when the 'learned' individual was simply someone who knew a lot of things. In his mental data banks lay precious stores of facts and figures. He could impress and amaze by bringing them out for public inspection. Nowadays information pure and simple is superabundant. Everyone has rapid access to all the data they need by means of computers. Anyone can appear learned with the help of an electronic companion. But not everyone can manipulate that information skilfully. A keen student may soak up facts fed to him like sausage filling from a lecturer, but unless that teacher goes on to point up the relevance of this information, how it fits together, how it might be adapted for future use, then he has done nothing at all to educate. Having access to hard fact is in itself nothing to do with wisdom, appreciation, subtlety, judgement. These have to be learned, improved and tested.

So too does creativity. Here is another skill that can be learned. How, though, is it to be taught? Should 'Creative Thinking' be put on the school timetable alongside Geography and French? What textbooks would be needed for such a course, were it ever to exist? And what kind of tasks would be set?

One researcher who has addressed these questions is Dr Roger Gehlbach of the Instructional Psychology Research group at Simon Fraser University, Canada. Starting from the assumption that 'creativity is a relatively ordinary skill', Dr Gehlbach points out that teachers tend to provide 'opportunities to be creative' in schools (and he is thinking chiefly of primary schools) rather than provide genuine instruction in the creative process. Moreover, these opportunities to be creative are almost invariably limited to the visual arts and written composition. 'These are important observations,' writes Gehlbach, 'for they constitute the substance of the reason why conventional approaches to the development of children's creative skills have generally failed.'

What is wrong with these conventional approaches is that they are wholly rooted in what is controlled and predictable. When anything is taught in school there is a three-stage process involved. First, learners are exposed to a specific body of knowledge or a skill to be acquired; they then practise this; and finally they provide some kind of feedback to the teacher by way of a task or a test. If all has gone well then the learner should reach a predictable end-point, by passing the test or displaying the skill on a given task.

With creativity it is different. The outcome or product of a piece of creative learning cannot be predicted. It is, says Gehlbach, 'virtually by definition, not specifiable in advance'. This makes the conventional system of setting a task to be mastered extremely difficult. What is the child to be exposed to initially? How does he or she practise being different?

Secondly, there is the question of the kinds of creative task to be worked on. As we have seen throughout this book, there is more to creativity than producing works of art or musical compositions or imaginative literature. There can be creativity in engineering, economics and ecology as well as in human relationships and self-awareness. These are just as important as the fine arts. Indeed it could be argued that 'the kind of creativity demanded and practised in the sciences, engineering and everyday technology is much more important to the future of society and to the lives of our children than that required to make a sculpture or clay pot.'

If we are to put creativity on the curriculum, then it has to be a broad-based subject. It would have to deal with such issues as hunger and overpopulation, with ecology and environmental pollution. It would have to be problem-centred and not limited to the art room or English class.

Suitable creative tasks

In order to display creativity a child would need to be confronted with a task that allows him or her freedom to arrive at a non-specific, non-predicted conclusion. However it is no use being totally free or 'open' in the manner of presentation. No child would be more creative in the presence of a teacher who says, 'I'm going to make a clay figure of whatever I choose. Just watch.' On the other hand, the teacher must not be so specific in the exposure phase that the learner merely copies everything slavishly and in great detail, so that the product or outcome is totally predictable. Dr Gehlbach sums up the dilemma thus: 'The problem in the design of instruction in creative processes has been one of finding a middle ground between the vagueness of total openness in task design, which renders creative activity by learners virtually "unteachable", and detailed end-product specification, which closes off the possibility of creative function by reducing the opportunities for novel thought.'

One way round this is to set tasks that are familiar to designers and engineers in which the end product is not specified but its function is. An engineer designing a giant telescope, for instance, is not given a brief that says 'Mount the instrument on a set of rollers with servo motors to tilt it in several directions'. Usually the task is set as an astronomical problem: 'We want to be able to carry out this kind of observation in the northern sky'. Likewise a composer or a poet laureate is not told what to write but for what occasion the composition is intended. Such problems – which Dr Gehlbach calls 'functional tasks' – can also be set for children and older students as a way of employing and honing their creative skills.

Here is one such task that might be given to explore a student's creative use of electrical circuitry.

A *'functional task'* for students of electricity

Exposure   The teacher ensures that students have basic knowledge of circuits and introduces the idea of placing switches in series.

Practice task   Find a way to design a circuit so that sometimes (a) changing only one switch will turn a light off or on and at other times (b) changing two switches will be required.

Materials   Cigar boxes, wire, toggle switches, light sockets and bulbs.

Feedback   Children operate their boxes and the circuits give feedback (i.e., they either work or they do not).

In this problem the task is introduced by a general data base of knowledge, and followed by practice tasks that impose – as with the telescope engineer – certain constraints. The criteria for completing the task are also clear-cut; both teacher and student will know if and when the task is finished. However there is a creative element here in that there is no single correct solution. The learner has an opportunity to devise novel ways of solving the problem. Below are two more examples of functional tasks, one for developing creative writing and art appreciation, the other drawing/painting and poetry appreciation.

A *writing and art appreciation task*

Exposure   The teacher guides a class discussion of several well-known portrait reproductions (e.g., Rembrandt, Vermeer), in which the focus is on the painter's ability to represent aspects of the subject's personality.

Practice task   Children are presented with an array of 12–18 reproductions of portrait paintings of men, women and children. They are asked to write a story utilizing at least three of the portrayed persons as characters.

Feedback   Children present their stories to peers who attempt to identify which portrayed persons are included in the story.

Art and poetry appreciation task

Exposure   The teacher guides a class discussion of how painting and drawing can be used to illustrate central ideas in poetry, using illustrations from children's and adult literature (e.g., Wildsmith, Picasso, Miró).

Practice task   Children are presented with an array of 6–12 poems about the same animal (e.g., Robert Louis Stevenson, Chukovsky, Lewis Carroll on crocodiles). They are asked to make a drawing or painting which illustrates only one of the poems.

Feedback   Children show their drawings to peers who attempt to identify which of the poems has been illustrated.

Source; Journal of Creative Behavior, vol. 2, no. 1, 1987.

Provided then that tasks are correctly devised and solutions are both challenging and amenable to a variety of novel solutions, it is possible both to systematize creative thought in the classroom, and to do so over a broad range of subjects.

The older learner

We can extend the idea of creativity training in schools and colleges to any other context. The same principles and approaches will yield positive results. The difficulty often lies in how creativity training is packaged. At the Manchester Business School, Tudor Rickards from the Creativity Programme realized that there is a good deal of cynicism among practising senior executives over the value of creativity training for the manager on the job. It is, they feel, valid for 'trainees' but not for those of some standing. On further examination, though, Dr Rickards saw that this 'credibility gap' could be closed if and when managers saw how creativity training related expressly to their own everyday problems.

So often they are faced with 'creativity' sessions that amount to little more than trying to solve what seem like childish puzzles. For example:

'A manager made what appeared to be a doodle on his desk-top notepad. He was actually writing down a message in two different ways, but one straight line was left out (he became distracted momentarily by a high-pitched whine from his refrigerated drinks cabinet). Can you find a possible way of re-establishing a message written in two different but equivalent ways?'

9 50

10 10 10

Now such games, though enjoyable, hardly seem relevant to the cash-flow difficulties of a multinational firm or the delays in processing raw materials before they enter the production line. What Tudor Rickards found in the case of 23 executives of director level taking a management course was that busy businessmen and women are certainly interested in innovative, valuable and original ideas. They want to initiate change and work within a more open intellectual climate. They are not regimented conformists. In short, they are keen to practise and promote creativity, but only when it relates directly to their own pressing problems, not as some abstract training exercise.

Our creative future

'I believe that in 100 years' time,' writes Dr Edward de Bono, 'people will look back with incredulity at the primitive nature of our thinking systems today. They will regard it as astonishing that the idea of teaching thinking skills in schools should ever have been a pioneering idea. Problems like Northern Ireland and the Falklands and disarmament will have obvious solutions. Is this a science fiction utopia?' Utopian or not, Dr de Bono's insistence on the value of teaching thinking skills – including creativity training – does have the merit of being based on a firm research foundation. As we have repeatedly seen throughout this book: by the deliberate application of certain strategies, given sufficient motivation, we can all improve our creativity ratings.

A less certain way of injecting greater amounts of creativity into human society in the future is that proposed by the industrial tycoon cum social theorist Robert Graham. He set up the Repository for Germinal Choice – better known as the Nobel Sperm Bank – to collect and freeze the sperm of Nobel Prize-winning scientists and offer this allegedly valuable seed to intelligent women with infertile husbands. The reasoning is obvious. Nobel Prizes are given to people of unusual levels of creativity. Since all intellectual attributes are determined to some degree by one's genetic inheritance, it should in theory be possible to pass down creativity in one's genes. And the vehicle for genetic inheritance is the male sperm. Or so

Robert Graham and other sperm bankers argue. Actually Graham is not in the business of producing great numbers of potential Nobel laureates as such: 'We're happy,' he once said, 'to produce competent, creative, interesting people who might otherwise not be born.'

Now the idea looks attractive, at least to women wanting babies with exceptional minds or musical skills. Indeed, it looks as if there is something to be said for it on scientific grounds, in that intelligent people tend to produce intelligent offspring. But here we run up against the drawbacks of 'selective breeding'. Quite apart from their Hitlerian undertones, such attempts to steer intellectually useful genes into the next generation have to confront some substantial difficulties. Will the child be brought up in an environment that will nurture and develop his or her creativity? This does not necessarily mean a home where all the activities are geared to furthering the would-be prodigies' talents. After all, some of the great works of literature have been bred in dissatisfaction, even despair – the grit in the oyster that ends up as a pearl. What will be the balance of the mother's genes to those of the father? Remember the retort of Bernard Shaw when asked by a handsome woman whether the two of them might have a child that would possess her looks and his brains. Shaw pointed out, not irrelevantly, that their offspring might end up with his looks and her brains.

No. If the immensely valuable resource of creativity is to be more widely exploited, there is no need to queue for service at the sperm bank. The resource is within all of us. We have only to recognize that to move one great step towards benefiting from it.

Some pioneers are already showing us the way. One such individual is the Israeli educationalist Reuven Feuerstein. In the 1950s, Professor Feuerstein was given the job of assessing the intelligence of young Jewish immigrants arriving in their thousands by boat for entry into Israel. Conventional tests sorted the youngsters out into groups but only, he decided, on the basis of what they had already learned, not what they could learn. Moreover the standard IQ tests put a label on a child that is difficult to shift later in life, however much aptitude or ability may begin to surface.

The experience led Feuerstein to devise a new kind of teaching designed not just to impart facts but to get a child to think. Called Instrumental Enrichment, it tackles thinking in much the same way that a shot putter sets about improving his distances, breaking down his action into grip, stance, balance, timing, footwork and so on. Michael Delahaye describes IE thus:

> By intense, quasi-Talmudic, sessions of question and answer, they (the children) are made aware of the discrete stages that are essential for the evaluation of experience – perception, analysis, comparison, classification, hypothesis, synthesis – all those complicated mental processes that most of us acquire naturally but which many children, often those later categorized as 'low achievers', miss out on.

In practical terms this means that children taught by Feuerstein's methods spend a lot of time solving problems which draw on these skills of pattern identification or classification and so on. They become familiar with the meaning of sophisticated terms such as 'stratagem', 'hypothesis' and 'parameter', using these frequently in the search for solutions. The teacher is not there to fill their heads with knowledge of a factual kind but to light the fire of enthusiasm and to fuel their self-confidence. It works. Children do gain self-esteem and a degree of verbal fluency that they previously lacked. They impressively demonstrate advances in their ability to process fresh experience. Thus they are in a sense more intelligent and more capable of meeting the creative challenges thrust before them in resolving problems.

So far IE has been limited to the special lessons of a 'Skills Programme'. There has been no attempt to transfer it to other disciplines such as physics or history to see whether it enhances performance there as well. It may not do so. But it is an experiment in teaching people to think that is well worth trying.

Artificial aids

The history of mankind's mastery over the environment is replete with cheating. We are not the biggest, the fastest, the most ferocious, but we are the best at making devices that enable us to defeat the animals that are. If we want to dig a big hole, we don't spend generations breeding specialists with enormous muscles: we build a mechanical digger. If, then, we can augment our abilities in these physical fields, why not in the world of mental capabilities? Could we build ourselves a machine that would do our thinking for us? One that would come up with novel and original solutions to our problems? One that would be creative? Certainly, those working in artificial intelligence think so.

In 1956 researchers in the infant field of AI held a conference at Dartmouth College in New Hampshire. To the conference came Allen Newell and Herbert Simon, then working in Pittsburgh. They brought with them the results of a new computer program they had written. It was called the logic theorist, and its purpose was to prove theorems in mathematics. In fact it was able to come up with proofs for some of the work in Whitehead and Russell's *Principia Mathematica*. This could be interpreted as displaying intelligence of a high order, but more to the point one of the proofs the machine found had not been seen before. By most of the criteria we have been using to define creativity, then that program had been creative.

Nearly fifteen years later, not much progress had been achieved towards making a creative machine. Then in the late 1960s, Harold Cohen, an English artist working in California, started a series of projects to see if he could program a computer to paint and draw. He wrote what was in effect an expert program for drawing. Using his own expertise he derived a set of about 300 rules which the computer followed. They gave the computer knowledge of the nature of light and shade, of the connections possible between lines, the difference between an open and a closed structure, and so on. The computer directed a motor-driven cart which carried a pen. The position of the cart was known to the computer. Drawing proceeded in a staccato fashion. The cart would draw a feature. The program would then decide what to do next on the basis of a pseudo-random number generated inside the machine. The computer was also aware of the things it had already drawn, and took them into account when deciding what to draw next. The machine proved to be capable of generating unique pictures. They contained some of the randomness you might expect from the scheme outlined. But they also contained recognizable figures, including birds, clouds and mountain ranges.

DRAWING BY AARON

It is possible to argue that the creativity in Aaron is the result of interpretations placed upon the picture by the person looking at it. Even so, Aaron's products are undeniably original. Cohen has followed Aaron with other machines. Aaron 2 draws with a more confident look.

DRAWING BY AARON 2

Source: Donald Michie and Rory Johnston, *The Creative Computer*, Penguin, 1985, pp. 142–3.

Cohen's lead has stimulated others to write drawing programs. They have usually tried to dispense with the random element of Cohen's work, and specify all the elements which will go into the finished picture. They attempt to produce novelty by exploiting the complexity of the systems they can generate. Again, this form of computer creation seems to beg the question – or perhaps to illuminate it. If all the elements are defined, then can there be true originality, or creativity?

The computer scientists argue that there can. The combination of the elements in previously unthought-of ways is what constitutes the novelty. If they are right, then perhaps the information processing model of creativity (Chapter 3) might have some truth in it. Certainly, as eminent a brain scientist as J. Z. Young believes that we operate according to a set of programs built into our brains. In his book *Programs of the Brain*, he argues that the way to understand how the millions of cells in the brain all work together is to suppose that there exist programs which direct their activities. These programs are written in our genes and our brains. Some are concerned with 'housekeeping' – making sure that we eat, or sleep, or breathe. Others are to do with language, with the process of growing up, with dying. But for Young, the most important are to do with our mental life, things such as: 'thinking, imagining, dreaming, believing, and worshipping'.

Young's programs are in some sense like the programs that drive computers, but they also have differences. Most computer programs are rigidly defined. Young's have the capacity to alter, to mutate, or even to generate new programs. And it is the generation of new programs which constitutes the act of creation. Young believes that the brain is built in such a way as to seek 'satisfaction' to the senses from the world around it. And one of the strongest sources of satisfaction is aesthetic experience:

The activities that go to the creation and enjoyment of works of art are . . . quintessentially those by which the brain, working every day as a creative agent, synthesizes input from the world to make a satisfactory life. This is why I say that for human societies the creative, aesthetic and artistic activities are among the most important things that we do . . . The creations and satisfactions of art include and symbolize both our individual acts of perception and the expression to others of what we perceive. These are the very brain actions that give us the power of communication by which we obtain all the rest, food, shelter, sex, and social life.

If Young is right, then in principle it should be possible to write a program that mimics every aspect of human creativity. At what point mimicry becomes duplication, if at all, is a judgement we will leave to you.

This difficulty had been recognized in the early days of AI. In 1959, L. A. Hiller and L. M. Isaacson in their book *Experimental Music* saw the problem clearly:

> The question of whether computers will ever be 'creative' in the sense that we speak of creative composing is rather similar to the problem of whether they 'think'. Also we might ask: 'What is meant by the term creative?' Being 'creative' would seem to depend at the very minimum, like 'thinking', on having the computer operate on a self-sustaining basis, and 'to learn from experience'. Moreover, it seems that what we first consider strokes of insight and manifestations of 'creative thought' are, once they are analysed and codified, and particularly, codified to an extent that they can be processed by a computer, no longer 'creative processes' in the usual sense.

One thing this statement reveals, apart from Hiller and Isaacson's love of inverted commas, is a common thread of thinking about computers, and in fact about human abilities in general. If we can formalize it, put it in a form computers can use, runs the argument, then somehow it will lose the creative essence, the nebulous, incomprehensible human inspiration that determines true creation. But the possibility that their output will be sneered at has not deterred others in just about every field of artistic endeavour from harnessing computers. There are computer-generated poems, novels, sculptures, music, animated films, and in one of the most unusual projects, kinetic sculpture. Perhaps the most bizarre manifestation of kinetic sculpture was the device built in

1970 by Nicholas Negroponte, working with a group at the Massachusetts Institute of Technology. The device was called Seek. It used a computer to drive an overhead crane to pick up and arrange 500 cubes. The machine was given an element of randomness – its arrangement was not ordered and regular. A number of gerbils were then released into the world made by the cubes. They would knock them over. The computer would then drive the crane to pick them up again and re-arrange them. Apparently, Seek was intended to demonstrate that computers can respond to the random occurrences that happen in the real world. 'But is it art?' asked the critics. Most of the gerbils did not think so. They died.

It seems reasonable to assume that sooner or later a machine will be made that can pass a sort of creative version of the Turing Test. Take the work of a suitably programmed computer. Place it in an exhibition alongside the creations of acknowledged, and perhaps not so acknowledged, human artists. Do not identify the computer art as owing its genesis to the workings of a machine. If it can stand comparison with the best that people can produce on the basis of judgements made by human critics, then we would necessarily have to call it creative work.

Those days are probably some way off. In the meantime, though, computers can offer rather more restricted but potentially equally useful help to artists. In particular, the introduction of computerized systems for composing and performing has removed a number of constraints on musicians. It is now possible, for example, to compose music one note at a time and instruct the computer to remember it. Once the basic notes are in the machine's memory, they can be manipulated in almost any way. They can be shifted in pitch, or in the length of time they occupy. Indeed it becomes possible to play assemblies of notes so quickly that a human musician could not possibly perform them. The original sound of the note can be changed into almost anything else, so a piano sonata can be played by the sound of cows lowing, or dogs barking. Musicians who have these systems attest to their value. They remove the technical constraints and allow the composer to concentrate on melody, rhythm and harmony. They allow something new to be produced.

It would be surprising if similar systems do not come into being for every field of art. In the same way that oil painting is impossible without oil paint, perhaps the next generations of artists will strive for their creative insights with the help of a computer and a colour display. It would be rash to dismiss such a prospect as spelling the end of human creativity simply because it exploits the virtues of a machine rather than of human eyes, fingers and brains.

Another area where computers might enhance human creativity is in the supply of information. Throughout this book, it has become apparent that good ideas do not spring from a void. They need background knowledge to feed upon. The time is coming when it will be possible to obtain access to immense knowledge bases from a home computer terminal. Already it is possible to buy an electronic dictionary. The size of a smallish book, it contains the spellings of tens of thousands of words. The words can be retrieved in a number of ways – one of which requires only some knowledge of how the word might be spelt. Imagine being able to find quickly and easily not only the spelling of a word, but all the words that mean roughly the same. An electronic thesaurus as an aid to creative writing! As the cost of electronics comes down, it will become possible to have electronic encyclopedias on every subject imaginable. And once the knowledge is there, the power of the human mind to make connections will take over. We could be not far away from a time when everybody, given the will to create, will have the knowledge to do so.

End of the search

In the final analysis the search for the keys to creativity turns out to be astonishingly straightforward. Once we discount the seductive red herring of inexplicable genius and recognize the immensely creative nature of normal, everyday thinking, we begin to appreciate not a rare handful of 'gifted' individuals but each and every person around us. We become aware that the precious quality of creativity is in truth common currency; that aspects of character, personality and above all motivation are what convert a base metal to pure gold.

Remember, too, that the judgement and sensitivity displayed by creative people are not infallible. Not only do eminent artists and scientists have their failures – which of course everyone always forgets – they sometimes dabble outside their major area of interest in quite sterile activities. From being astute and perceptive thinkers they can become gullible and uncritical. J. S. Bach believed that numbers had mystical properties; Mozart was convinced by the symbolism of Freemasonry; Charles Dickens aligned his bed directly on a north–south axis to avail himself of the alleged benefits of the earth's magnetic properties; while Benjamin Franklin – common sense personified one might think – belonged to a mystical sect that believed in the transmigration of the soul.

Conversely, someone who has never displayed any creativity at all, in the conventional sense of having musical talent, problem-solving ability, skill in interpersonal relationships and so on, may turn out to have a surprising faculty for making sense of the world in the broadest terms. He or she may see with penetrating clarity a grand design or pattern in what many of us regard as the absurdities of human existence. Such people may appreciate an order and a purpose in a universe that often looks random and hostile. They may, in short, become attuned to a greater divine reality and discover religion. This too is a sort of creative act: to impose sense on nonsense, meaning on fruitlessness. And, perhaps more than any other act of creation, it requires no special gifts or aptitudes.

To be creative ultimately is to be nothing more than human. To be human is of necessity to be creative.

Answer to puzzle on p. 201.

9 50
10 TO 10

BIBLIOGRAPHY

Aleksander, Igor, and Burnett, Piers, *Thinking Machines*.
Oxford University Press 1987

Blakemore, Colin, *Mechanics of the Mind*. Cambridge University Press 1977

Changeux, Jean-Pierre, *Neuronal Man*. Oxford University Press 1985

De Bono, Edward, *De Bono's Thinking Course*. Ariel Books/
BBC 1987

De Carlo, Nicola, *Psychological Games*. Facts on File Inc.
1984

Feynman, Richard P., *Surely You're Joking, Mr Feynman!*
W. W. Norton & Company Inc. 1985

Gardner, Howard, *Frames of Mind*. Paladin 1985

Gazzaniga, Michael S., *The Social Brain*. Basic Books 1985

Gould, Stephen Jay, *The Mismeasure of Man*. W. W.
Norton & Company Inc. 1981

Greene, Judith, *Thinking and Language*. Methuen 1975

Gregory, Richard (ed), *The Oxford Companion to the Mind*.
Oxford University Press 1987

Hudson, Liam, *Contrary Imaginations*. Methuen 1966

Hunt, Morton, *The Universe Within*. Harvester Press 1982

John-Steiner, Vera, *Notebooks of the Mind*. University of
Mexico Press 1985

Koestler, Arthur, *The Act of Creation*. Hutchinson 1964

McCorduck, Pamela, *Machines Who Think*. W. H. Freeman 1979

May, Rollo, *The Courage to Create*. Bantam 1985

Michie, Donald, and Johnston, Rory, *The Creative Computer*. Penguin 1985

Minsky, Marvin, *The Society of Mind*. Heinemann 1987

Ornstein, Robert, *Multimind*. Macmillan 1986

Ornstein, Robert, and Thompson, Richard F., *The Amazing Brain*. Chatto & Windus 1984

Rothenberg, A., *The Emerging Goddess*. University of Chicago Press 1979

Searle, John, *Minds, Brains, and Science*. BBC 1984

Sternberg, Robert, *Human Abilities*. W. H. Freeman 1985

Storr, Anthony, *The Dynamics of Creation*. Penguin Books 1983

Taylor, David A., *Mind*. Century 1983

Vernon, P. E. (ed), *Creativity*. Penguin Books 1978

Weisberg, Robert W., *Creativity*. W. H. Freeman 1986

Young, J. Z., *Programs of the Brain*. Oxford University Press 1978

INDEX